Commendations f[...]

"*Leadership by the Book* is both prac[...] :al leadership is waning. The way Dr. Jon[...] ith scriptural reference is the type of guide all leaders need. I am convinced that in order to produce better leaders we have to start by 'the book.' This piece gives us the frame-work to do the work of leadership development."

—*Kenneth Chapman Jr, executive pastor, Life-Changing Faith Christian Fellowship, Frisco, TX*

"We live in a milieu devoid of Christian leadership as demonstrated in Scripture. Dr. Jones calls Christian leaders to rethink the biblical understanding of kingdom leadership. This work offers a comprehensive definition of kingdom leadership from a biblical, theological, and exegetical framework. Dr. Jones reminds us that Christian leadership is more about being with Jesus than doing for Jesus."

—*David Gambo, Reverend A. E. and Dora Johnson Hughes Chair of Christian Ministry and assistant professor of Christian ministry, Oklahoma Baptist University*

"Building on Jesus Christ as the risen king, Jones guides readers from the Old Tes-tament to the New Testament about developing leaders scripturally through a holis-tic approach. Kingdom leaders are chosen, appointed, and authorized through Jesus Christ. This book should be required reading for any emerging leader who desires to influence their followers in a biblical, effective manner."

—*Daryl D. Green, Dickinson Chair of Business at Dickinson College of Business, Oklahoma Baptist University and author of* Impending Danger: The Federal Handbook for Rethinking Leadership in the 21st Century

"Dr. Jones provides us with scholarly and practical frameworks on cultivating king-dom leaders. This book is outstanding for those who are on missions and will enor-mously help Christian leaders in any cultural setting. I will be using it to cultivate local Christian leaders in Asia."

—*James Kang-McCann, founder and director of Amerasian Christian Academy and senior pastor at Global Vision Chapel*

"If you're in search for a helpful guide on Christian leadership, you must read Galen Jones's *Leadership by the Book*. Jones grounds the concept of leadership in Scripture and from here, he develops some essential qualities and characteristics worthy of attention and emulation. Whether you're a pastor or business owner, this book offers helpful insights and practical guidance for you."

—Scott Pace, vice president for undergraduate studies and associate professor of preaching and pastoral ministry, Southeastern Baptist Theological Seminary, dean of The College at Southeastern

"With vivid imagery, clear biblical exposition, and inviting prose, Dr. Galen Jones offers a work pregnant with leadership principles awaiting delivery by God-chosen leaders. Dr. Jones serves as a delivery coach who, in *Leadership by the Book*, carves from the Bible truths applicable to the daily lives of leaders who lead others to Christ. This practical yet scholarly work guides leaders from wishful thinking about effective leadership to purposeful possession of invaluable leadership skills."

—Robert Smith Jr, Charles T. Carter Baptist Chair of Divinity, Beeson Divinity School

Commendations for Hobbs College Library

"This series honors a wonderful servant of Christ with a stellar lineup of contributors. What a gift to the body of Christ! My hope and prayer is that it will be widely read and used for the glory of God and the good of his Church."

—*Daniel L. Akin, president, Southeastern Baptist Theological Seminary*

"This series is a must-have, go-to resource for everyone who is serious about Bible study, teaching, and preaching. The authors are committed to the authority of the Bible and the vitality of the local church. I am excited about the kingdom impact of this much-needed resource."

—*Hance Dilbeck, executive director, Baptist General Convention of Oklahoma*

"This series offers an outstanding opportunity for leaders of all kinds to strengthen their knowledge of God, his word, and the manner in which we should engage the culture around us. Do not miss this opportunity to grow as a disciple of Jesus and as a leader of his church."

—*Micah Fries, senior pastor, Brainerd Baptist Church, Chattanooga, TN*

"The best resources are those that develop the church theologically while instructing her practically in the work of the Great Commission. Dr. Thomas has assembled an impressive host of contributors for a new set of resources that will equip leaders at all levels who want to leave a lasting impact for the gospel. Dr. Hobbs exemplified the pastor-leader-theologian, and it's inspiring to see a series put out in his name that so aptly embodies his ministry and calling."

—*J.D. Greear, pastor, The Summit Church, Raleigh-Durham, NC, and former president, the Southern Baptist Convention*

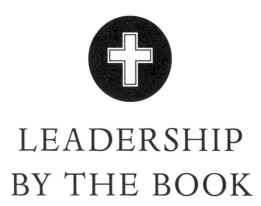

LEADERSHIP
BY THE BOOK

HOBBS COLLEGE LIBRARY

LEADERSHIP BY THE BOOK

*Cultivating Spirit-Led
Kingdom Leaders*

GALEN WENDELL JONES

HEATH A. THOMAS, *Editor*

OBU

ACADEMIC

BRENTWOOD, TENNESSEE

ISBN: 978-1-0877-5401-7

Dewey Decimal Classification: 303.3
Subject Heading: LEADERSHIP / JESUS CHRIST—TEACHINGS / DECISION
MAKING

Printed in the United States of America
28 27 26 25 24 23 VP 1 2 3 4 5 6 7 8 9 10

Dedication

*In the past four months, my life has completely changed for
the better. Up to this time I have had no children; although I
longed for them, they were not forthcoming. I had resolved,
through many tears, pains, and prayers, that the sovereign
Lord has determined—no children for Galen and Cathy.
Nine days before my initial deadline for this volume was due, I received
an enigmatic email from a man in Korea named James Kang McCann.
He wanted to know if I was Galen W. Jones who was stationed in
Korea many years before. Not really reading the email, I simply
answered in the affirmative, thinking he was someone from my old Army
unit, and gave him my updated contact information.
Much to my great surprise, I discovered that
he was not in my old unit nor in the military at all.
The man informed me that he was,
in fact, the pastor of a young man named Kang Soo-il
and he had reason to believe that I was Soo-il's biological
father. Whoa, and WOW!
Thank you, Ancestry.com!
In one sweeping motion, I learned that I have a son—a most
wonderful young man—my Soo-il. Needless to say, my life has
changed in so many wonderful ways since knowing my son.
I especially thank him for bringing new life to
me and his new mom, Cathy Renee.
So, as it is in my heart to do, I dedicate this book
to my dear sweet son, who is now
the delight of my life and an added source of strength to Cathy and me.
Soo-il, I speak the words that our heavenly
Father commanded Moses to speak to
Aaron and his sons, saying, "May the Lord bless you and protect
you, may the Lord make his face to shine upon you and be
gracious to you; may the Lord look with favor on you
and give you peace—Shalom. In this way
they will pronounce Yahweh's name
over you, and he will bless you."
Num 6:24–27
I dedicate this book to our son, "Naui Gippeoum 'My Delight.'"*

Contents

Acknowledgments

To God be the glory—to the King Eternal. Your loving-kindness has been my food all the days of my life. I am completely indebted to King Yeshua, my risen Lord and Savior, for his uncompromising grace and mercy. I will never forget the days of my folly when your love was near me, but I was far from you. From heaven, you came and rescued me (Col 1:13–14).

I am grateful for all the family members who have come before me and left a grand Christian heritage for me. I am especially thankful for my grandfathers, William Warren Jones Sr. and Laken Cosby Sr., who through the worst of times for black men lived as giants in their generation. And to my grandmothers, Momma Sue and Momma Cosby, who walked faithfully by their husbands as beacons of the Messiah's light and personal intimacy.

To my dear sweet beautiful wife Cathy Renee, your love for me has been one of the precious gems of my life—you perfectly embody Prov 31:10. If I lived a thousand lives, I would marry you in each one of them. Thank you for being a barometer for my soul and an anchor of spiritual wisdom and fortitude. You are truly a gift from the Holy One (Prov 19:14). To my son Soo-il, you are my strength and my song—you have captured my heart.

I have been blessed to have many great pastors in my life who have taught me the Word of God and modeled biblical leadership. Thank you for your love and guidance. My spiritual walk is enhanced by the late Dr. James Earl Massey. Dad Massey, as we call him, left an indelible mark on my heart that is still carrying me in life long after he has gone. Many people around the world are familiar with

Dr. Robert Smith Jr. (potentate of preachers). I have the awesome pleasure of knowing you as my father in ministry. Your loving care for me and Cathy is only surpassed by your love for Yeshua. Cathy and I are indebted to you for the wisdom, guidance, prayers, and spiritual leadership you have provided for us and for me personally. Thank you for caring.

A few years ago, Heath A. Thomas, then dean of the Hobbs College of Theology and now president of Oklahoma Baptist University, invited me to contribute a volume on leadership to the Hobbs College Library. This volume is the answer to his gracious invitation. I am blessed to know Heath as my former dean, and I am doubly blessed to know him as my brother and friend. Thank you for your friendship. Equally, David Wesley Whitlock and his wife, Dana, have been for Cathy and me true friends and fellow travelers in our journey with the Messiah. Thank you, David; you are special to me. Gratitude must also be expressed to my brothers and colleagues at Samford University's Christian Ministry Department—Scott Guffin, Kevin Blackwell, and J. D. Payne—you inspire me. And to my students I've shared the learning journey with—I hope you find the risen King in this book.

I wish to thank the many dear friends who have contributed to this work in one way or another. To Emily Kuykendall, thank you for all you have done to edit and help me think and present my ideas and passion for the risen King. Bob Drovdhal, our work together is reflected in the wisdom you inspire. To my Brother Dr. J. Robert White, you have always been an inspiration, mentor, and friend. Thank you for helping me theologically and personally as you guided me along the way.

And to my parents, William and Christie Jones. Your efforts to raise me with a conscience for the Kingdom of God and with the ability to see all people as God's image bearers has made me into the man of God that I am today. I gleefully anticipate the time when the Lord allows us to see, to laugh, to love, and to live with one another forever.

About the Library

The Hobbs College Library equips Christians with tools for growing in the faith and for effective ministry. The library trains its readers in three major areas: Bible, theology, and ministry. The series originates from the Herschel H. Hobbs College of Theology and Ministry at Oklahoma Baptist University, where biblical, orthodox, and practical education lies at its core. Training the next generation was important for the great Baptist statesman Dr. Herschel H. Hobbs, and the Hobbs College that bears his name fosters that same vision.

The Hobbs College Library: Biblical. Orthodox. Practical.

Introduction

*On the evening of that first day of the week,
when the disciples were together,
with the doors locked for fear of the
Jewish leaders, Jesus came and
stood among them and said, "Peace be with you!"
After he said this, he showed them his hands
and side. The disciples were overjoyed
when they saw the Lord. Again Jesus said,
"Peace be with you! As the Father
has sent me, I am sending you." And
with that he breathed on them
and said, "Receive the Holy Spirit. If
you forgive anyone's sins,
their sins are forgiven; if you do not forgive them,
they are not forgiven."*
John 20:19–23, NIV

I remember so well the moment the King came into my heart. I was ten years old attending Vacation Bible School at Zion Baptist Church in my hometown of Cincinnati, Ohio. My older brother Aaron responded to the minister's invitation. Back then, whatever

Aaron did, I did. So, as he strolled down the aisle, I followed him—but about halfway down the runway, I felt the risen savior stirring in my heart and calling me to himself. By the time I reached the altar I was in tears repenting before the King of glory, hoping he would forgive me of my sins and allow me to live with him forever. I do not remember the Scripture the minister quoted back then, but as an adult, I am certain that I was saved by God's glorious grace and that he has given me work to do (Eph 2:8–10).

About two years later, sitting at my mom's dining room table, my cousin Kevin Wayne Cosby and I were talking about the things of the Lord. Kevin knew from the ripe old age of six that he would be a preacher. The Lord was moving in my heart, and I was not sure what was going on when suddenly Kevin slammed his hand on the table and shouted something like, "God is calling you to preach." Fear and joy simultaneously flooded my soul because I knew God was in fact calling me to serve him. By the age of fourteen, I was preaching in my community to all who would listen. It was in this season that I began to learn to submit to King Jesus as my Lord for the first time.

The Gospels of Matthew and John appealed to me then as well as today. Many of my sermons come from these texts. When one recognizes Jesus as the King, it involves much more than making a simple theological claim. The recognition that he is King has implications for a person's entire life. Simply put, to know him is to experience the transformation that comes with his power and authority to wipe away all our sins (John 20:18–23; Acts 3:18–20).

Christ Jesus: The Risen King

I understand now why I have such a passion for Christ the risen King. The Gospels present Jesus as the King (see Matt 2:2; 27:37b) more than any other picture of him. "The Fourfold Ministry of our Lord," appendix 119 in *The Companion Bible* compiled by E. W. Bullinger, can help us grasp the veracity of this claim of Christ's kingship. Bullinger contends that the greatest subject matter of the four Gospels revolves around two main subjects, (A) the *King* and (B) the *Kingdom*. Each of these subjects can be broken into two separate sub-topics—(1 and 2) the acceptance and rejection of the King, and (3 and 4) the acceptance and rejection of the Kingdom. The following information is from Bullinger's notes in appendix 119.

Four Main Subjects of the Gospels

1. **Proclamation of the Kingdom:** Matt: 125; Mark: 7; Luke: 42; John: 132 = 306.
2. **Proclamation of the King:** Matt: 347; Mark: 295; Luke: 204; John: 18 = 964.
3. **Rejection of the King:** Matt: 134; Mark: 110; Luke: 409; John: 248 = 901.
4. **Rejection of the Kingdom:** Matt: 263; Mark: 138; Luke: 171; John: 209 = 781.

Scripture makes clear, through the volume of the subject matter, that the King and the Kingdom are of utmost importance. The Kingdom is referred to 1,088 times, and the King is referred to 1,865 times.[1] My sense of awe and respect for the King is partly due to what I learned from Bullinger's appendix, but more importantly to simply reading the pages of Scripture over the course of my lifetime and

---

[1] For a full complement of this subject matter, see appendix 119, "The Fourfold Ministry of Our Lord" in *The Companion Bible,* the Authorized Version of 1611 (KJV). Notes and appendices compiled by E. W. Bullinger (Grand Rapids: Kregel, 1999).

recognizing that the coming King is the messianic hope of the children of Israel and all who long for his return.

I believe that the mission of God's people is to be examples of what it means to live dramatically for him, to worship the King, and to be *on mission,* sharing the reality of who he is with all of humanity. The drama of Scripture and the power of being conscripted into his service is summed up in the statement in the Johannine Great Commission. That is, in the same way that the Father sent the Son, so the Son sends God's people (John 20:18–23). Moreover, his followers are *called, equipped* and *authorized* by him to do the transformative "greater works than these" he gave us to do (John 14:12–14; see Eph 2:10).

The drama of the Bible and the present assignment of God's people is to be on mission*,* presenting him in his fullness as the risen King of glory. Obedience to the call to be on mission as followers of the King is the process of God's people sharing *The God News* with God's world. The God News is a reclaiming of what the term "Good News" once conveyed—the transformative truth of Jesus. By reframing the gospel with a new title, The God News, I hope to center our attention and leadership endeavors on the risen King. The reallocated term *The God News* serves this book by elevating the power of experiencing the living God through Scripture and through moments of profound faith, and then moving forward in obedience to the mission of sharing the news of King Jesus. Accordingly, the joy, responsibility, and ultimate goal of the body of Christ is the sharing of The God News.

My definition of *The God News* is designed to provide a new perspective to the ancient yet relevant gospel of Jesus. What my perspective offers is the age-old ingredients of the Good News, with an emphasis placed on the transformative announcement that Christ Jesus is the risen King. Further, I hope to provoke new questions

4

about the ancient story so that wherever the King is experientially presented, all people can flourish.[2] Wherever and whenever the crucified risen King is made known, his power—his rule, his authority—and his forgiveness of sins transforms people and communities.[3]

Some Clarifications and Definitions

For the sake of clarity, some terms to establish are: Transformation, the Announcement, Forgiven-Forgivers, and Kingdom Leaders. While some of these terms may seem familiar, I find it necessary to clarify my usage to more fully establish how they contribute to the role of leadership in light of the all-transforming God News of Jesus Christ.

Declination versus Transformation
Over the last several decades, the church has experienced rapid decay. Researchers such as Thom Rainer, Ed Stetzer, and the Pew Forum report that the church in North America has seen a severe decline.[4] Evangelicals are split on virtually every topic in a most

---

[2]   See Ross Hastings, *Missional God, Missional Church: Hope for Re-evangelizing the West* (Downers Grove: IVP Academic, 2012).

[3]   My argument is based on the exegesis of John 1:14; 14:15–24, where Jesus promises that the triune God will take up residence in his people. We carry the presence of the most high God in the same way that the children of Israel carried the presence of God in the ark of the covenant (Lev 26:12; 2 Cor 6:16).

[4]   "In U.S., Decline of Christianity Continues at Rapid Pace," Pew Research Center (Washington, DC), October 17, 2019, https://www.pewforum.org/2019/10/17/in-u-s-decline-of-christianity-continues-at-rapid-pace/.   Ed   Stetzer,   "How Should We Think About Declining Denominational Numbers?," *The Exchange* (blog). Thom Rainer, "Major New Research on Declining, Plateaued, and Growing Churches from Exponential and LifeWay Research," *Church Answers Featuring Thom Rainer* (blog), March 6, 2019, https://churchanswers.com/blog

ungodly manner. The divisions among us are especially egregious along racial and political lines. The preaching of Jesus Christ crucified and raised from the dead is passé at best and completely irrelevant at worst. As an educator in the field of Christian ministry and leadership, now at two different Christian liberal arts universities, I encounter many young people. The vast majority, many of whom come from "Christian homes," have little to no real knowledge of the tenets of the Christian faith—and what knowledge they do have seems to be at the early elementary school level.

Let me say emphatically, something is terribly wrong! Generally speaking, the gospel has of late suffered unbelievable disregard.[5] It no longer seems relevant to the church and its veracity is irrelevant to most in secular society. Jesus is widely regarded as just another religious leader with one old message among many. The New Testament's regard for the exclusivity of Christ as the Savior of humankind is dismissed as intolerant, arrogant, and prejudiced. Western society, and the world for that matter, is becoming more and more pluralistic, and the ideas of postmodernity have saturated our culture and infiltrated the church. Judeo-Christian values and standards are constantly disputed, while the distinguishing dimensions of a Christian worldview are seriously questioned. In our postmodern world, the need to regain a righteous hearing of the gospel in the public forum is at an all-time high. This is why I believe that sharing The God News ought to be the focal point of Christian leadership.

N. T. Wright, in his book *Simply Good News*, argues that the Good News is not simply good; rather, it is transformative.[6] The

---

/major-new-research-on-declining-plateaued-and-growing-churches-from-exponential-and-lifeway-research/.

[5] N. T. Wright, *How God Became King: The Forgotten Story of the Gospels* (New York: HarperOne, 2012), 5–10.

[6] N. T. Wright, *Simply Good News* (New York: HarperOne, 2015), 16.

Good News, as Wright suggests, affects the whole storyline of one's life and the larger storyline of entire communities. The announcement of the death, burial, resurrection, ascension, and return of Jesus clearly seems to no longer be significant, much less transformative. As the church, we must seek to restore the gospel, The God News, to its proper place of transformational influence in our lives. To do so, the church and Christian leaders must live on the edge of two distinct extremes—a declining church and the rise of secularism—so that church life functions as God intended it to: like a lightning rod to postmodernity. I argue along with Wright and T. D. Alexander that the Good News is relevant for all people at all times—however, in the past several decades, the presentation and announcement of the Good News has lost its savor. Because of this, throughout this volume, I refer to the gospel as The God News.[7]

The Announcement
The God News as I define it is the announcement and experiential presentation of the King. This includes his virgin birth, his perfect life, his death on the cross, his bodily resurrection with the demonstration of his transformative power (i.e., power to forgive sins), the promise of the Spirit, and his imminent return. Further, the concept of leadership to be discussed in this book is wholly contingent on the notion that the transformative power of The God News is the announcement of King Jesus in all his glory, from Genesis to the Revelation![8] Specifically, the announcement I refer to is from Acts

---

[7] T. D. Alexander, *The Servant King: The Bible's Portrait of the Messiah* (Vancouver: Regent College, 2003).

[8] As some are no doubt thinking there are other important facets of the gospel, such as Christ's ascension, let me be abundantly clear—what I mean by "presenting him" is through both specific and natural revelation to include proclamation and the demonstration of the power and presence of the Holy Spirit. Further it involves

2:38, "Repent, Peter said to them, and be baptized, each one of you, in the name of Jesus the Messiah for the forgiveness of your sins, and you will receive the gift of the Holy Spirit." This is the transformative announcement that can change the world.

A brief examination of the Johannine Great Commission (John 20:18–23, 26) begins with the risen King making the announcement that he is ascending to the Father. The King commands Mary Magdalene to make the announcement to his disciples. Her encounter with the risen King—that is, her new experience of him—led her to obediently proclaim, "I have seen the Lord" (John 20:18, NASB1995). That same day, the risen King makes himself known to the disciples (19); he sends them in the same manner that the Father sent him (21); he proleptically imparts them with the Holy Spirit (22); and he authorizes them to pronounce the forgiveness of sins (23). Additionally, John 20 concludes with Jesus performing many other signs and miracles in their presence (30–31).

Forgiven-Forgivers and Kingdom Leaders
The God News *transforms* the disciples, and they in turn become world transformers, or what I call Forgiven-Forgivers. Part of the transformative power of The God News is the authority granted by the risen King to his followers to forgive others of their sins. Forgiveness from the King is not only transformative; it is restorative. As Forgiven-Forgivers, we make the transformative announcement that we too have seen the risen King—he has forgiven our sins. Moreover, the process of Christ perpetually transforming us is a continual process throughout the remainder of our lifetime. As the King's

---

warning people of the judgement to come (Pss 19; 23; 24; Matt 24:14; Mark 16:14–20; Rom 1:1–32; 2 Cor 5:20; Rev 1:1–22:21).

Forgiven-Forgivers we are called into his service as ambassadors of reconciliation (2 Cor 5:19–20), or what I call Kingdom Leaders.

Kingdom Leaders are "incarnational followers of the King whom he *appoints with authority*, *equips [for service]*, and *sends* to *influence* [all] people to pursue the Father's will; and who in their lives and ministries display the *active indwelling presence* of the Holy Spirit."[9]

The Road Ahead

A word is in order regarding the structure of this volume. To begin with, this is a book on Christian leadership, as is provided in the definitions regarding The God News and Kingdom Leaders. It presents the concept of leadership in two major parts. Part 1 addresses my definition of The God News and develops infrastructure for thoughtful consideration of Jesus as the Messiah of Israel and his fulfillment of God's promised plan, her long-awaited Messiah.[10] It also discusses the personal relationship with Christ that is necessary for a person to qualify as a Kingdom Leader. Part 2 addresses what we do with the personal relationship we have with Christ when it is applied to Kingdom leadership. We must seek to apply the personal connection we have with Christ to reaching a lost world. Additionally, one of the primary aims of this work is to provide my perspective of Christian leadership through the lens of what I call Kingdom Leadership, as seen through the motif of Christ Jesus the risen King.

---

[9] On the definition of Kingdom Leaders, see my article: Robert R. Drovdahl and Galen Jones, "The Times They are a-Changin': Christian Leadership Over the Last 40 Years," *CEJ* 17, no. 3 (December 2020): 579.

[10] Walter C. Kaiser Jr., *The Promise-Plan of God: A Biblical Theology of the Old and New Testaments* (Grand Rapids: Zondervan, 2008).

Chapter 1 surveys the notion of Jesus—the risen king—being the fulfillment of the promise of God given in Gen 3:15 and the covenant made with Abraham in Gen 12:1–3. First, in chapter 2, I examine Abraham and his relationship with God as the template for what it means to be called into leadership. Second, Abraham's life is used as a model for detailing our role as servants of the Lord. And lastly, I explore his life as a representation of what it means to be a worshipper and follower of God. Chapter 3 goes into a detailed explanation of my definition of The God News, particularly addressing the idea of experiential presentation of the King. Chapter 4 is a bridge to part 2. In this chapter, the paradox of biblical leadership is presented. I also provide my definition of Kingdom Leadership as the group of individuals who are defined as incarnational followers of Christ Jesus whom he appoints with authority, equips for service, and sends to influence humanity to pursue the Father's will. These individuals also should demonstrate the active indwelling presence of the Holy Spirit in their lives and ministries.

Part 2 moves on to the broader canvas of fleshing out the meaning of Kingdom Leadership. Chapter 5 addresses being *appointed* by the Lord and *authorized* for action as a Kingdom Leader. Chapter 6 explores how leadership is intended to be cultivated in the hearts of upcoming leaders as well as furthered in our own. Chapter 7 discusses the need for Kingdom Leaders to develop other leaders to be sent, just as Jesus has clearly sent us. Lastly, chapter 8 reflects on the application of this book as a Kingdom Leader; it explores how we connect our deepest intimacy with the Father to a role of servitude toward our flocks and other rising leaders.

A foundational aspect of leadership in the Kingdom of Christ Jesus is that it is a Spirit-led endeavor. Biblically, leadership has always been and will always be a Spirit-led experience. In the post-modern world, it is crucial that leaders not only are led by the Holy

Spirit but also demonstrate the indwelling presence of the Holy Spirit. So, with that said, a theology of the incarnation of the Holy Spirit is necessary in seed form within the lives of the community of believers and particularly in the lives of those who are called to be leaders. By using the theological word *incarnational,* I do not want to incite controversy or come up with some new off-the-wall doctrine. My intent, as my friend Malcolm Yarnell suggests,[11] is to reengage our imaginations creatively through a fresh understanding of the Holy Spirit to allow him the proper place in our hearts as leaders. My goal in introducing a theology of the indwelling (incarnational) presence of the Holy Spirit is to spur conversation and inspire a renewed focus on the role and place of the Holy Spirit in the fulfillment of the words of Jesus in John 14:12–14 and 17:1–26.[12]

After we've traversed this road together, after all the twists and turns, my heart's desire for you is that you know the risen King in

---

[11]   I owe this insight to a personal conversation with Malcolm Yarnell, director of the Center for Theological Research and professor of systematic theology at Southwestern Baptist Theological Seminary.

[12]   The words of Jesus in John 14:12–17 and 17:1–26 are some of the most compelling words that have ever been spoken and recorded. No matter what one considers to be the meaning of Jesus's words in John 14:12–17 (whether he meant "greater works" in magnitude due to more of his people doing what he did or whether he meant greater in scope because of the indwelling presence of the Spirit) is a concept that demands reconsideration. The reality is (John 17:1–26) that the Father and the Son are in perfect union according to Jesus's high priestly prayer. Moreover, according to this text it is Christ's will that his body—endowed (rather) *incarnated*—by the Holy Spirit would share in that very union of life and purpose. The notion that the Holy Spirit is incarnated in the body of believers is not nearly as far-fetched as might be thought. Gordon D. Fee demonstrates quite convincingly that the giving of the Spirit is the eschatological fulfillment of Christ's incarnation. Fee, *God's Empowering Presence: The Holy Spirit in the Letters of Paul* (Peabody, MA: Hendrickson, 1994), 803–915. My suggestion is that where Fee uses the phrase "empowered by the Spirit," I suggest the phrase "incarnated by the Spirit" as a means of reinvigorating and deepening our conversation about the role of the Spirit not only in theological discourse but also as fulfillment of the Great Commission.

his fullness. It is my prayer that this book influences the way the King equips you as a leader and as you train up other leaders under you. I want us to all come to know Christ better and gain deeper appreciation and anticipation for his return to take us home to be where he is. Amen.

CHAPTER 1

The God News of the King

I will put hostility between you and the woman,
and between your offspring and her offspring.
He will strike your head,
and you will strike his heel.

Genesis 3:15

The promises of God are the surest words ever spoken. Gen 3:15 is commonly referred to in theological circles as the *proto-euaggelion* or the first *messianic promise* in Scripture. Here we witness for the first time one of the many places in the Bible where God declares with great emphasis an *I will statement* that carries the reader from one Testament to the next. In the beginning, God creates the man and the woman in his image (Gen 1:27). The creation of humankind is truly an act of intimacy. In effect, divinity kisses dirt—he brings the man to his lips and breathes the breath of life into him, and man becomes a living soul (Gen 2:7). In contrast to the somewhat sterile creation account given in Genesis 1, the Genesis 2 account depicts a deeply personal and intimate connection between God and the first human.[1] The notion of divine-human intimacy also

---

[1] Alexander, *The Servant King,* 16–17 (see introduction, n. 7).

serves as a template for the sacredness of male-female intimacy, which is made full when we give intimacy back to the Holy One. The cyclical nature of intimacy was designed by God to be an ongoing, everlasting cycle between the Holy Creator and his beloved. We can refer to this as the *plan of life*.[2] This perfect environment between the lover and his beloved is presented beautifully in the purity of the nakedness of the first couple (Gen 2:25).

The original intimacy that permeates Eden, in which the Holy One and his beloved interact with one another in complete harmony, is disrupted by the serpent when Adam and Eve fall to temptation, eat from the tree of the knowledge of good and evil (3:6), and thereby rupture the intimacy provided by God. No longer will mankind experience perfect relationships—humanity will painfully coexist with one another. Pain and tension will pervade every aspect of human life. Adam and Eve are expelled from the garden of Eden (3:22–24). In light of all this tragedy, God provides hope—he makes the first announcement of The God News when he passionately, intensely, and prophetically declares to the serpent and his beloved, "*I will* put hostility between you and the woman, and between your offspring and her offspring. He will strike your head, and you will strike his heel" (3:15, italics added).

The events of Genesis 3 provide much fodder to discover God's mood as he unequivocally says what "*I will do!*" God displays a great deal of emotional content in Gen 3:15, as this is his first

---

[2]   Life, I argue, is the overriding theme of Genesis and consequently the entirety of Scripture. Particularly as it leads to eternal life provided in the life, death, and resurrection of Jesus. Genesis is authoritative and sets the foundation, theologically, for the Holy Writ. The early narrative unit of Genesis has something to say theologically regarding the purposes of God for mankind. God's purpose for creating mankind was that man would live with God forever. Death and the ravages of the fall are extremely important and cannot be ignored; nevertheless, the plan of life, I suggest, is significantly more important.

announcement of The God News. It is the first announcement that the Savior will come, transform, and change everything—it is the announcement, albeit in proleptic form, that God himself will come, in the seed of the woman, to reverse the effects of the fall. It is the very announcement made in Luke 2:11 by the angelic host fulfilling every *I will* of God in the Old Testament, especially the *I wills* concerning the coming of the great King. As the story unfolds, the woman, Eve, seems to have optimism at the birth of Cain—that she has given birth to the seed that the Lord had promised,[3] that God has fulfilled what he said he would do.[4]

> "Listen, Israel; The Lord our God, the Lord is one. Love the Lord your God with all your heart, with all your soul, and with all your strength. These words that I am giving you today are to be in your heart." (Deut 6:4–6)

---

[3] Commentators such as E. W. Bullinger suggest that Eve considered that God had in fact allowed her to give birth to the promised seed. Bullinger contends that the Hebrew of Gen 4:1 where she exclaims, "I have gotten a man from the Lord," is '*ish eth Jehovah*, meaning "a man even Jehovah." (See notes from Bullinger on this text in *The Companion Bible,* 8.) Bullinger further suggests that the fulfillment of this first announcement is directly connected to the words of the angelic host in Luke 2:11—that the seed of the woman has come in the birth of Jesus—thus fulfilling The God News of Gen 3:15. Additionally, the notes by commentators of the English Standard Version Study Bible (Crossway, 2008) suggest that Eve at minimum had optimism at the births of Cain and Seth (see notes on verses 4:1–25 on pp. 57 and 59), that the works of the serpent will yet be overthrown by her offspring.

[4] One of the most important and powerful studies one can engage in is completing an in-depth study of all the text in Scripture that utilizes the phrase "I will." By studying this phrase, one will discover not only the importance of knowing God's promises for the collective good of his people but also the severity of knowing, experientially, his judgment for disobedience. For example, see Gen 12:1–3; 17:5–8, 16–21; 18:14 and 22:15–18. See also, Exod 3:6–15; 6:1–8 and Jer 29:10–14; 31:1–3, 27–34 (first announcement of the new covenant), and lastly, but not limited to Ezek 34–36:36 and 37:5–14.

An Afrocentric Canonical-Leadership Hermeneutic

The presentation of The God News is an all-encompassing endeavor—one that involves our entire being—that is, our whole soul. Theologians of the African diaspora throughout the world are known for capturing the intellectual-emotional side of the Scriptures uniquely through what I call Afrocentric Canonical-Leadership Hermeneutics.[5] Most notable among these great theologians are the late James Earl Massey, Clarence Jordan, E. K. Bailey, and Gardner C. Taylor, as well as eminent theologian preachers such as Robert Smith Jr., Claybon Lea Jr., Ken Fentress, Celucien Joseph, and Charlie Dates. What makes them great theologians and great leaders is their ability to rightly ascertain the intellectual depth of the text, as well as their ability to capture the emotional content of the text. Black theologians, like the ones mentioned here, are to be considered on par with other theologians of renown—particularly, with those who espouse the concept of the drama of Scripture.[6]

---

[5]   Afrocentric Canonical-Leadership Hermeneutics is the process uniquely inspired by African American theologians and preachers that engages one's entire soul and spirit in the process of preaching. The Bible calls us to love God with all our heart, mind, soul, and strength (Deut 6:4–5; see Matt 22:37–40). I submit that Kingdom leaders lead from this same mode of conscientious-sensorial leadership. That is, leadership in Christ's kingdom involves one's entire being. Leadership then is the displaying of a leader's love relationship with the Holy One and loving others; that is, as he or she loves God. Conscientious-sensorial leadership is adapted from Henry T. Mitchell. See note on Henry T. Mitchell below regarding conscientious-sensorial preaching. See also Clarence Jordan, *The Cotton Patch Version of Matthew and John* (Piscataway, NJ: New Century, 1970).

[6]   In this vein, see the work of Kevin J. Vanhoozer, *The Drama of Scripture: A Canonical Linguistic Approach to Christian Theology* (Louisville: WJK, 2005). Craig G. Bartholomew and Michael W. Goheen, *The Drama of Scripture: Finding our Place in the Biblical Story* (Grand Rapids: Baker Academic, 2004). And the edited volume by David Gibson and Jonathan Gibson, *From Heaven He Sought Her:*

Part of the strength of the theologians of the African diaspora is that they were able to make an intellectual, emotive, theological, and symphonic connection to the Scripture through Abraham, Moses, and the exodus so that there is a confluence of our whole being which informs our ecclesiology, missiology, soteriology, and leadership. Simultaneously, the Black theologian makes the intellectual, emotive, theological, and symphonic connection as the people of God so that the trajectory of our leadership hermeneutically carries us personally from Gen 12:1–3 to the second great exodus (Isa 11:11–12) through to Rev 22:21.[7]

It is important to recognize that biblical leadership involves one's entire being—including the whole scope of human emotion. The notion of whole-self involvement in the delivery of the text is found in what Henry T. Mitchell, well-known as the father of African American preaching, construes as conscientious-sensorial preaching.[8] Mitchell's view of conscientious-sensorial preaching argues that preaching happens when all the preacher's senses are engaged in the delivery of The God News so that the hearer can engage all of their senses in the reception of it.

Definite Atonement in Historical, Biblical, Theological, and Pastoral Perspective (Wheaton, IL: Crossway, 2013).

[7] African American theologian Robert Smith Jr. suggests that the African American, and others of the African diaspora, connect wholistically to the proclamation of the Word of God as the fruit of our oppression. Smith argues that that God infuses a kind of intimacy into the soul of the oppressed in a manner that is special and distinct from what he does in the life of those who have not been systematically oppressed. Robert Smith Jr. and Charles T. Carter, interview by author (Birmingham: Samford, 2022).

[8] See Henry H. Mitchell, *Black Preaching: The Recovery of a Powerful Art* (Nashville: Abingdon Press, 1990).

Mood-Voice Relationship

One of the avenues of biblical interpretation I teach is what I refer to as the mood-voice relationship. Simply put, the mood-voice relationship denotes the deep emotional content of what the text of Scripture is communicating so that one experiences a conscientious-sensorial (emotional) content of the Author. Yahweh, the Holy Creator of the universe—the Author of Scripture—is an emotive God. The text of Scripture, I suggest, reveals the emotion of God.

This hermeneutic seeks to discern emotional specificity by asking questions of the text such as what might be the sound of the speaker's voice and what might be the drama of Scripture discoverable in a particular pericope. And, given the reality that the text of Scripture was written according to the literary and social conventions of the ancient Near East, it is important to capture the setting of life of the persons and places contained in the text. We ascertain emotional specificity historically from the text—for example, who is speaking, who is the audience, and how they are experiencing what is happening. Moreover, the mood-voice relationship seeks to discover not only what is being said but also the tone with which the speaker is communicating their message. It also seeks to uncover the desired response, through acts of obedience, but also the feelings one has in response to the command of God. We seek to discover and identify the *Sitz im Leben* or the "setting in life." This is done by discovering the internal realities and the emotional conditions that permeate the people in Scripture.

For instance, I regularly ask my students how God's voice sounded in Gen 1:3. I also ask what his emotional content was when he said, "Let there be light." I always make sure both male and female students stand up in class and speak as if they were God. Obviously, no one knows how the Creator sounds and what his emotional state was when he first spoke—we especially do not make doctrinal conclusions based on the mood-voice context—but it helps us to grasp the *Sitz im Leben* in Scripture when we can experientially place ourselves in the text.[9] Genesis alone is filled with stories of intrigue and drama that rival any modern "who done it?" Think of what it would involve reenacting such episodes as Jacob's (and his mother's) deception of Isaac and Esau. Or what about the rape of Dinah and the response of Simeon and Levi, her brothers?

Place yourself in the story of Judah and Tamar. Here, God kills Judah's sons because they act wickedly. What was Judah feeling when God killed his sons? God slays one of Judah's boys, specifically for not fulfilling the levirate vow toward Tamar. By way of intrigue, Judah goes into what he thinks is a prostitute and is not able to pay her for rendered services; he unwittingly impregnates Tamar and demands that she be burned to death when he learns of the pregnancy, but subsequently learns of his own unrighteousness and her righteousness (38:6–26). Simply put, to miss the emotional content of these stories in Genesis is to miss a significant portion of Scripture's context. Will Kynes, a noted Old Testament scholar, offers that "grasping the emotional content of the Text is crucial to properly understanding it. As well, the Hebrew language is filled with emotional variants in the words themselves."[10] If we are missing that

---

[9]   Here I draw on two concepts from Walter C. Kaiser's principlizing method and what he calls the ladder of abstraction. The reader of Scripture must build a bridge from the text to life. See Walter C. Kaiser, "A Principalizing Model" in *Four Views on Moving Beyond the Bible to Theology,* ed. Stanley N. Gundry and Gary T. Meadors (Grand Rapids: Zondervan, 2009), 11, 24.

[10]   Conversation with Will Kynes, January 6, 2021, Samford University. For a broader investigation of the Hebrew language and variant means to translate it, see also: Suohkrie Kesolenuo, "Abraham, Israel and The Nations: The Implications of Abraham's Blessing for The Nations," (MTh thesis, MCD University of Divinity, 2015), https://repository.divinity.edu.au/entities/publication/f3da14ff-81b6-4f9d-b6ef-1d379388df4a/full.

much of the emotional context in the first book, which sets the stage for the rest of the Bible, then we risk going astray for the remainder of the Bible and missing the drama that continues to this very day!

Yahweh's Rule in the Old Testament

We now focus our attention on the most important issue for our purposes—that Yahweh is the sovereign Ruler of the Old Testament and is the same King in the New Testament. Moreover, the entire Old Testament displays Yahweh as the great King. Jesus's announcement that "the kingdom of heaven has come near!" is the culmination of The God News (Matt 3:2). The idea of Yahweh as the sovereign Ruler of Israel and the entire universe is not new to the New Testament. Kaiser emphasizes this point in his monumental work, *The Promise-Plan of God: A Biblical Theology of the Old and New Testaments*, where he spells out ten characteristics of the promise-plan of God as one promise from Genesis to Revelation.[11] The promise that Yahweh is the sovereign King of all the universe is explicit throughout the Old Testament. In the Psalms, we read, "The LORD has established his throne in the heavens; And his sovereignty rules over all" (103:19, NASB1995; see also 96:10; 97:1). Both Isaiah and Jeremiah, without equivocation, write that "Heaven is [Yahweh's] throne and the earth is [his] footstool" (Isa 66:1, NASB1995); and he, Yahweh, is "King of the nations" (Jer 10:7). The book of Daniel is noteworthy for exclaiming the sovereign rule of the Most High and the Ancient of Days who inherits an everlasting kingdom. Daniel proclaims, "His kingdom is an eternal kingdom, and his dominion is from generation to generation" (4:3b, see also Dan 7; Zeph 3:15–20; Zech 9:9, 14:8–9, 16–17, 20; and Mal 1:14).

---

[11] For an expanded list of "Ten Characteristics of the Promise-Plan of God," see Kaiser, *The Promise-Plan of God,* 19–25 (see introduction, n. 10).

Hope for the Future Coming of the Great King

All through the Old Testament the Holy One provides glimmers that the hope of Israel, the great King, will come based on the profound fulfillment of the first and last of Yahweh's *I wills*. A few shining glimmers of Israel's hope for the great King are seen in Deut 17:14–20, the story of Ruth and the offspring born to her, and the covenantal promise of Yahweh to provide a "forever King" to sit on Israel's throne in 2 Sam 7:11b–16, 25–29.

We see clearly through the Minor Prophets that the Holy One continues to be prophesied of—the Hope of Ages will soon come to Israel. We read further of the promise of Solomon and the (few) righteous kings who follow. First and Second Kings and all the messianic promises of God found in the Psalms (e.g., Pss 1–2; 8; 22–24:7–10; 40:6–10) show from Gen 3:15 that God in truth is fulfilling his word of promise.

The King Made Manifest

The sure attestation of the Gospels—Matthew, Mark, Luke, and John, in conjunction with the book of Acts—is that Jesus of Nazareth is the risen King of glory, God himself in the flesh (Matt 2:2; 27:37; Mark 1:1; 15:38–39; Luke 2:8–14; 23:38; John 1:14–34; 20:18–31; and Acts 1:1–8).[12] The New Testament's overarching theology centers around Jesus's life and ministry as King of the kingdom of God; his preaching and healing ministry point to the reality that he supersedes nature and rules over demons.

For instance, in Mark 5:1–20, Jesus encounters a man who lives in the tombs. The man is wild and fearsome to the people from

---

[12] Thomas F. Torrance, *Incarnation: The Person and Life of Christ* (Downers Grove: IVP Academic, 2008).

the town. Scripture recounts that "no one was able to restrain him anymore—not even with a chain" (Mark 5:4). The man cries out to Jesus, "What do you have to do with me, Jesus, Son of the Most High God? I beg you before God, don't torment me!" (Mark 5:7). The demons inside the man ask Jesus to cast them into the herd of pigs nearby instead of casting them out of the region. Jesus commands the demons to do so, and the man is set free. This story reveals the power of Jesus over dark forces and the demons' acknowledgment of Jesus's lordship.

Additionally, Jesus himself and others identify him as the Son of Man and Son of David (Mark 8:32; Luke 18:38). In Matthew 9, as Jesus is healing a paralytic, he says, "'For which is easier: to say, "Your sins are forgiven," or to say "Get up and walk"? But so that you may know that the Son of Man has authority on earth to forgive sins'—then he told the paralytic, 'Get up, take your stretcher, and go home'" (vv. 5–7). As he displays his power over physical healing, he also asserts his identity as the prophesied Son of Man.

Brian Vickers, in his article, "The Kingdom of God in Paul's Gospel," asserts that Jesus of Nazareth is the one true living God incarnate and the thrust of Paul's theology. He writes, "At the heart of Paul's concept of the kingdom of God is the risen enthroned Christ. Without suggesting yet another 'center' of Paul's theology, it is safe to say that the reality of the reigning Christ is a key component of Paul's theology."[13]

The Rule and Reign of the Risen King

Space and purpose do not allow me to cover the dramatic expanse of Old Testament history revealing how the seed of the woman

---

[13]   Brian Vickers, "The Kingdom of God in Paul's Gospel," SBTS *Journal of Theology* 12, no. 1 (Spring 2008), 52–65.

will become the Hope of Israel. With all the drama, murder, and intrigue found in the Old Testament, who would have thought God's announcement in Gen 3:15 would culminate in The God News of the New Testament? The transformative news consists of the One who died, rose from the dead, ascended into heaven, and is coming back again.

As leaders, it is essential to acknowledge the reign of Christ as Lord from the beginning to the end of Scripture because of the quintessential impact the truth has on the form of Kingdom leadership. In the kingdom of God, leaders are called to lead others from a submissive followership of Jesus. Leaders are chosen, like Abraham, Moses, and David, to be humble followers of Christ the King who point to the transformative truth of the gospel.

CHAPTER 2

The God News—Chosen to Be a Blessing

The Lord said to Abram:
Go from your land, your relatives,
and your father's house, to the land that I will show you.
I will make you into a great nation,
I will bless you, I will make your name great,
and you will be a blessing. I will bless those who bless you,
I will curse anyone who treats you with
contempt, and all the peoples
on earth will be blessed through you.
So Abram went, as the Lord had told him . . .

Genesis 12:1–4

T he life of Abraham shares with us a picture of what it means to be a Kingdom Leader. A Kingdom Leader consists of being both a true follower and a true worshipper of God. The call of Abraham is the direct response of the heart of God to the fall of Adam.[1] Moreover, Abraham embodies the characteristics God intends for those who are called into leadership.

---

[1]   Wright, *How God Became King*, 73–74 (see introduction, n. 5).

The call of Abraham matters to our overall understanding of what it means to be called by God, providing the foundational stones for all who are subsequently called into the Lord's service. One's calling is the result of the sovereign selection of God. The voice of the Messiah calls, and we who hear him as our Father Abraham did react with an *Immediate Radical Obedience Response* (IROR). The process of responding to the call can be varied, but two elements of response are universal. For one, all who are called respond to him in obedience—David is in the pasture tending sheep, Nehemiah and Ezekiel are in a distant land serving another king, Amos is in Tekoa functioning as an obscure sheepman, and Paul is a pharisee in hot pursuit of the followers of The Way. Second, each person called by God has a bona fide experience with him that carries him throughout his life. More will be said later concerning one's experience with the Lord; albeit, the outcome of a true call is always the same—complete and total submission to his will. As Bonhoeffer says, "When Christ calls a man, He bids him come and die."[2]

Immediate Radical Obedience Response

One of my former professors and mentors, and my father in ministry, Dr. Ronald E. Cottle, always described Christ's call to ministry by telling us young preachers: "When Christ *kaleos* you, he does so as the sovereign Ruler of the universe. Not some namby-pamby, soft-shelled man you see on television. No, No, No No," he would go on, affectionately exclaiming, "Boys, when Christ *kaleos* you, he kicks down the door of your heart, sits down on your seat of authority, raises his scepter, declares his right to rule you, and reminds you it is a privilege to be called. And our response to that call is the

---

[2]   Dietrich Bonhoeffer, *The Cost of Discipleship* (New York: Touchstone, 2018).

immediacy of action, not faith."[3] Citing Matt 4:18–22, Dr. Cottle regularly pointed out that the disciples acted in immediate obedience to the voice of the Messiah. The call to follow Jesus, he reminded us, is no mere mental ascent; rather, it involves one's entire being. Like Abraham, Isaiah, Peter, and Paul, our response is to be one of immediate radical obedience; or as Isaiah says, "Here am I, send me" (Isa 6:8b, KJV).

Abrahamic Leadership Principles

Abraham's life, as mentioned above, is foundational to understanding what it means to be called by the Holy One into his service. To truly grasp the elemental notions from the life and call of Abraham, we do not merely glean principles of leadership from the pages of Scripture. While this would no doubt have value, to grasp the veracity of Abraham's call, and our calling as well, it must be discerned through the mood-voice of our situation in life. Fundamentally, in the Hebraic sense, the notion of being *called* and or *calling* is first seen with respect to being drawn to the Great Shepherd with intimacy, to worship and adore him. Then, the Holy One extends to his beloved the privilege and authority to invite others into the same experiential relationship of intimacy, worship, and adoration. There, where we meet with him and experience him afresh, like Abram to Abraham and Jacob to Israel, we are changed to love him and serve him.

---

[3] Ronald E. Cottle, father, mentor, and friend to me and a host of other ministers, is founder of the Christian Life School of Theology and Beacon Institute of Christian Ministry in Columbus, Georgia. On many occasions in class and in personal relationships, Dr. Cottle would share passionately with his protégés the important realities of what it means to be called into service of the Lord. One of the most important facets of life, ministry, and Kingdom Leadership is to have mentors and fathers in ministry.

The Transforming Call of God

The call of God will place us in the life vortex of going from cognizance to cognitive dissonance and from dissonance to cognizance. It will take his chosen from hearing his voice to deafening silence and from silence to symphony. The journey of God will lead us into a life of becoming confused and becoming aware of the hand of God over and over again. The Holy One will regularly and systematically move us from one station in life to another—our whole lives (body, soul, mind, emotions, and spirit) are affected by his calling; sometimes we are shaken up, at other times broken—but through it all, he puts us back together again. Think of your life when God called you. If it was like mine, there were many emotions, thoughts, and concerns swirling through your heart—the call is exciting and scary and humbling, but the call of God is not sterile!

By studying Abraham's situation in life and his call to serve the Holy One, we can deduce principles of biblical leadership that are applicable to our ministry. Again, these principles are to be understood in the context of our whole being, not simply as notions drawn off of a page. They must also be considered in the context of the mood-voice of our life situation.

Abraham exemplified a life of consistently learning to provide the IROR after experiencing the prompting of God. Understanding your individual IROR as a leader is a commodity developed over time, as we observe in Abraham's life. Moreover, the following leadership principles flow out of our hearts, or rather they are issues of a heart that is drawn to the Messiah.

Principle #1: Leaders Must Know the Voice of God

After the death of Terah, God instructs Abram to go to the place that God would show him (Gen 12:1). Reading the text, there is no indication that the Lord tells Abram which direction to go and how far to travel. What we do know from the text is that Abram is directed to go to Canaan by way of Shechem. When he arrives there, God speaks to him again. He does not go south to Egypt, nor does he go north to Assyria, nor does he go east to India; rather, he goes west to Canaan. Abram learns how to be in the right place—where Yahweh wants him to be. Somehow, Abram knew to go in the direction that God wanted him to go. Our goal as leaders is to be able to rightly discern the voice of the Lord so that we, like Abram, know not only what direction God wants us to go but also the place he wants us to be.

I suggest, without being too dogmatic, that Abram was led by the Spirit from Ur of the Chaldees to the land of Canaan. In today's world, a leader must know how to follow the Spirit's leading, which in turn means a leader must discover how they hear the Spirit's voice. Jesus is clear that his sheep know his voice (John 10). There are many times that leaders hear the voice of the Lord in Scripture. In the New Testament, one example is when Lazarus (John 11:38–44) hears from the grave the voice of the Lord calling him back from death to life. In this respect, there is a sense of God calling us from a dead space back to a living one.

In what ways do you hear and discern the voice of the Messiah speaking to you? As a point of practicality, over the next few days or while you are reading this book, consider the ways you hear from the Holy One. Make sure to write them down.

Principle #2: Leaders Must Experience the Backside of the Desert

Once God issues the call, we respond to him with obedience. We hear his voice and discover the direction he wants us to follow. God quickly takes his chosen leaders through a time of preparation on the backside of the desert. By this I mean a season of difficulty that must be endured by the believer, whether physical, spiritual, or emotional. Every called leader must walk through the process of discovering what the Lord has for them on the backside of the desert! Think of it: virtually everyone in the biblical record spends time with God on the backside of the desert—even Jesus did. He spent forty days in the wilderness before he began his ministry on earth; there the angels served him, and Satan tempted him (Mark 1). The only leader in the Bible that I can think of who did not spend time with God in a solitary place of difficulty is Solomon. Consider the outcomes from his life and ministry—he had more wives and concubines than anyone in known history, Israel entered unprecedented idolatry as a result of his ministry, and the kingdom was divided under (or because of) his leadership. Do not neglect to spend time with God in dry places.

Hearing and Transformation

Abram is one who has a literal desert experience with the Father. Abram sojourns in the land of promise, and while there he hears the voice of God. He experiences the Lord's presence, and he is transformed into Abraham. The issues of Abraham's heart are dealt with until he arrives at the place where he becomes useful to God. He no longer lies about Sarah being his sister there. His courage is developed there. He experiences intimacy with the Holy One there. He learns greater levels of obedience there. What have you learned there, in your desert experience with the Lord? Are you hearing his voice? Are you being transformed? Are you allowing him to deal with the issues of your heart? The lessons learned on the backside of the desert can carry you through life and ministry.

Preparation for Ministry

Another purpose of the backside of the desert is to prepare us for life and ministry. He leads us there to humble us, and we learn the wonders of obedience and perseverance. The backside of the desert is your place for ministerial readiness. While we are in the desert place, the Holy One orients our lives to fulfill his calling. He molds a leader through divinely conforming three crucial domains of our lives:

1. **Humility:** For the leadership context, this is the critical and continuous quality of one's heart that exhibits trusting faith in and submission to the will of the risen King.
2. **Obedience:** For the leadership context, this is the critical and continuous quality of behavior that exhibits compliance of action from hearing the authoritative commands of the risen King.
3. **Perseverance:** For the leadership context, this is the critical and continuous course of action physically, psychologically, and morally resulting in walking with God despite difficulties, challenges, attacks, or opposition to doing the will of the risen King.

God, by his Spirit, does the wonderful work of giving all believers new hearts (see Jer 31:33–34 and Ezek 36:25–27); however, he puts those in leadership through the intricate process of conforming our hearts through special time on the backside of the desert. As the Spirit of God leads you to the backside of the desert to teach you humility, obedience, and perseverance, he provides five metaphorical tools to accomplish his goals. If you have been to the Holy Land, the picture of the Judean Wilderness immediately jumps to the forefront of your mind's eye. The desert and solitary places are some of Yeshua's favorite settings for training leaders. By the Spirit, Kingdom Leaders are provided with the instruments listed as follows:

1. a pick to break up the fallow ground, loosen rocks, and make corners
2. an ax to chop up old tree stumps that once represented a thriving ecosystem
3. a breaker bar to loosen dirt, rocks, and roots and to provide leverage for lifting and moving boulders
4. a shovel to remove dirt and make walls, corners, and connecting troughs
5. a wheelbarrow to move rocks, dirt, and old roots buried beneath weights on the surface of the ground

While there, with these items, the Holy Spirit says to his chosen, "Go, dig ditches!" The imagery here can be quite puzzling. Lord, did you say "go dig ditches here in the desert"? His plain and simple answer is, "Yes, I did." Now it is quite alright to ask questions, especially those that pertain to the dimension of said ditches. One thing I find to be true when questioning God is that the answer to the question of *why* is often not as forthcoming as we want it to be. It is not that the Lord doesn't want you to know the answer; it has much more to do with the reality that the first lesson to be learned is the lesson of obedience. The wise and obedient student asks, How deep, how long, how many, how wide do you want them, Lord? And to that, God speaks.

INTIMACY IN THE WILDERNESS
Sadly, one of the worst phenomena in the lives of too many Christian leaders is that they think the desert is a one-time experience in their lives. This could not be further from the truth. Often God will call you back to the desert just so you can spend intimate time with him. Many of us get too busy to spend intimate time with God. Yet, he woos us to the desert that we may know him—that we may not

forget him as our first love—and because he wants to speak tenderly to us there: "Therefore, behold, I am going to persuade her, bring her into the wilderness, and speak kindly to her" (Hos 2:14, NASB1995). God's leading us to the desert ought to be an ongoing life-giving experience for us, not a place of avoidance. Jesus himself regularly retreated to a solitary place to seek the intimacy of the Father. I challenge you to consider if you are avoiding the desert; if so, you may have already missed the point.

HUMILITY FROM THE DESERT

Another lesson in the desert is the joint lesson of humility and character development. You see, while you are out digging ditches and going through the hurts and pains of answering God's call, people are watching you. They are watching to see what you are made of. They are watching to see if you cut corners. And they are watching to discover if you are a trustworthy leader. Do you have the character that befits one of God's chosen?

Others, with a serious query, may wonder whether you have really lost your mind. Many will simply ignore you and consider what you are doing as irrelevant. And many, many more will scoff at you in laughter. The beautiful redeeming side of this is that through it all the Holy One is building character in you. He is working out of you things that offend and giving you the necessary prerequisites to handle what he is about to do through you for his glory. Part of the desert experience is to discover that you know deep in your heart that what you are doing is for his glory.

Interestingly, the simple and yet profoundly deep answer to the *why* question is "to catch the rain." Somewhere along the way while you are laboring—removing rocks and dead roots, moving dirt from one spot to another, crafting ditches—the Holy Spirit says, "I am going to send rain down; the rain is coming." Digging ditches on the backside of the desert produces hope in the face of adversity. It leads us to have radiant optimism balanced by necessary realism. It teaches us not to be ashamed. And depending on your obedience and vision, the ditches you dig will determine how much water will be retained—for his glory and the good of others. Remember that all those people who scorned your efforts or doubted your sanity may be the very ones who need a drink of living water from the oasis the Lord allowed you to build for his glory! One thing is for certain: the backside of the desert will reveal your character. It will develop character in you, or it will break you.

Principle #3: Leaders Must Be(come) True Worshipers

God created mankind to be in a love relationship with him. The Holy One kissed dirt and "man became a living soul" (Gen 2:7, ASV). God humbly chooses to first love us (1 John 4:10). Yahweh, out of his great love for us, provides everything we need to be in a relationship with him. He gives us the ability to respond to his love with love. Worshipping God is one of our most natural responses to God's love for us, and worship itself is an act of love. Abraham, throughout his life, is known as an authentic worshipper of the Almighty. Everywhere Abraham goes, he sets up altars for worship. For instance, Abram enters Canaan by way of Shechem at the oak of Moreh—the Lord appears to him, and the Almighty declares the covenant of promise. "So [Abram] built an altar there to the LORD who had appeared to him" (Gen 12:7b). The obvious inference is that Abram worships Yahweh there. As our father moved from place to place, he built altars to honor and worship Yahweh (see Gen 12:8; 13:4; 21:33; and 22:9). As you peruse the text, there is a pattern with Abraham; he is often noted for calling on the name of the Almighty, or as in Gen 21:33, he calls on the name of the everlasting God in the voice of one who loves and worships his God.

34

Abraham's life is filled with authentic and perpetual worship of the one true and living God! As you look through your life and love relationship with the Holy One, are you learning the lessons in principle #3? Is your life characterized as one who is an authentic worshipper of the Lord? Psalm 33:1 is a simple picture of one who is a worshipper of God: it says, "Rejoice [worship] in the Lord, you righteous ones; praise [worship] from the upright is beautiful." As leaders, we set the example for those we lead. Are you the worship leader in your home? Are you the worship leader in the community you live in? Are you the worship leader in the church or ministry you are called to? If not, take time to repent and ask the Lord to restore to you the beauty of lovingly worshipping him. Amen.

Principle #4: Leaders Must Be(come) Mature
We see in the life of Abraham that God calls him to loving servitude. Abraham demonstrates his love relationship with the Holy One by the way he serves God and others. Principle #4 is really connected with principle #2—God calls us to the backside of the desert to engage us in intimacy with him, and we learn much from those times of being intimate with him. God uses the backside of the desert to conform us to the image of his Son. He molds his chosen ones to the image of Christ by teaching us to learn from the deep pains of life. Most often it is the deep disappointments, the hurts, and even the tragedies of life that teach us the most about God's holiness, his sovereignty, and his manifold grace in order to shape our character.

The great lesson here is learning to appreciate (rather than tolerate) the sovereignty of God. It is also learning to appreciate the providence of God, especially as we and those we love experience hardships, sometimes debilitating illnesses, and even death. God's sovereignty and providence become a different story when it hits home in our hearts—when we are the ones who have lost family

35

and church members. Think of the heart-wrenching hurt that comes with the loss of a child or the pain that comes with not being able to bear children. I personally know this pain—my wife and I have been unable to conceive, with the one exception of becoming pregnant many years ago.

People who know me are aware that I have longed deeply for children all my life. We were several months along in our pregnancy when suddenly Cathy became sick, and it was clear that something was drastically wrong with our baby. I rushed her to the hospital only to find out that the baby was dying and there was not much that could be done. We were heartbroken but accepted God's will for our lives. I thought we could get pregnant again in due season. It has been thirty years now, and that season has never come. I thought I had gotten over the heartache of having no children and accepted that we just were not meant to have little Galens running around. Eight years ago, after seeing many people abuse and neglect their children, I had to have it out with God. I screamed, I yelled, I cried, I begged God to forgive me for whatever egregious wrong I had committed. On and on I pleaded with him to grant me this one thing—yet we have not had any children. What he did give me was peace in the process of life. Accepting the decree of the Lord can be tough—but it has brought me contentment and maturity in my life.

Another important milestone for me occurred several years ago. I had the opportunity to watch the experience of my spiritual father, Dr. Robert Smith, Jr., during the loss of his son, Tony. October 31, 2012, is a day he and his family will never forget. Tony was working in a barbecue fast-food restaurant in our hometown of Cincinnati, Ohio. That infamous night, a young man in a Halloween mask entered Tony's store and demanded money from the safe. For no reason at all, the robber shot and killed Tony while he was trying to oblige the young man. During my brother's funeral, I wondered who would do the honors of preaching the eulogy. There were many great men of God there. Much to my amazement, Dr. Smith himself preached his son's funeral. Not only had my spiritual father lost his son, but many years ago as a younger man, he had lost his first wife.

I will never forget the day he shared this experience with me as he passionately preached his son's funeral from the same passage he used preaching his young wife's funeral—Ezek 24:15–18. That day I was in tears as I drove him from Southern Seminary's campus to the Louisville airport. The Holy Spirit got us there as my eyes were too drenched to see clearly. Not only did Dr. Smith preach his wife's and his son's funerals, but he went to the prison where the robber was incarcerated and led him to a saving relationship with his Holy Redeemer, the Lord Yeshua.

One last story to make my point. A little over twenty years ago, my wife and I traveled to Ghana, West Africa. While there we visited Cape Coast Castle of the infamous transatlantic slave trade. The docent took us to the dungeons where the male slaves were housed until they were shipped to the Americas. I heard our host say that in that dungeon upwards of three hundred men were kept at one time. I looked at the space and could not believe that so many people could be packed in such a small space (thirteen paces one direction and sixteen in the other). Then she explained that if one of the slaves died in the dungeon he was simply left there to rot. Without hesitation I started raising my feet as I realized I was standing on the bodies of my ancestors. Later on we went to the girls' dungeon—most of the slaves taken were actually teenagers. Once again, horror struck my mind and heart as we were told that the young girls were raped practically every day. Still worse, there was a corridor that went to a set of stairs to the bishop's quarters through the back of the chapel. There the bishop, supposedly a church leader, would have his sport. We arrived back at our hotel on the ocean dumbfounded and dazed. I saw a rock sticking up out of the water about sixty yards away. I told Cathy I would be back. On that rock, I demanded that God tell me why. Why did and why do Black people have to endure so much? I cried, I yelled, I pounded my fist—I have to know, Lord, why? I thought of the millions of Africans who were tossed overboard—those who died in the middle passage. He never gave me the answer—he did however give me Rev 20:13, which says, "Then the sea gave up the dead that were in it. . . ." That text has a whole new importance for me now. He also put the song, "It Is Well with My Soul," in my heart, and I was able to come off that rock without hatred; I have learned to love and be content in him. Talk about sovereignty and providence. That's what the backside of the desert can do for you. The rawest parts of life can be the trials God uses to sharpen our endurance and make us mature believers, like James 2:2–4 says. Don't run from the desert—rather, when he calls you there, run to him in the wilderness.

Principle #5: Leaders Must Learn Contentedness

One of the pictures that emerges from the pages of Scripture regarding the life of Abraham is that he learns to be content with God, himself, and his station in life. He does not appear bothered by not having enough, nor is he moved in the wrong direction by having too much. As the apostle Paul reasons, "But godliness with contentment is great gain" (1 Tim 6:6). Paul also writes to the Philippians that he can find contentment "in any and all circumstances" because he learns to place his hope in Christ Jesus alone to strengthen him (Phil 4:10–23). Contentment is defined as "to be free from care because of satisfaction with what is already one's own."[4] Abraham displays

---

4   Greek word: *autarkeia*, noun form of the verb *arkeo*—primarily signifies to be sufficient, to be possessed of sufficient strength, to be strong, to be enough for a

a lifestyle of contentment with God. Part of the biblical reality for those in covenant relationship with the Holy One is that he provides everything: "For we brought nothing into the world, and we can take nothing out" (1 Tim 6:7).

CONTENTEDNESS OF POSITIVE CONFLICT RESOLUTION

As the story of Abraham's life continues, a time comes when the land cannot support both his and his nephew's burgeoning livestock and households. In Genesis 13, we see Abram returning from Egypt; Lot and all of his possessions are with him. They arrive in the space between Bethel and Ai—the place where Abram had built an altar of worship to the Almighty: "But the land was unable to support them as long as they stayed together, for they had so many possessions that they could not stay together, and there was quarreling between the herdsmen of Abram's livestock and the herdsmen of Lot's livestock" (Gen 13:6–7).

An important lesson to be learned on the backside of the desert (hopefully early on in ministry) is how to resolve conflict in a positive manner. The plain sense of the text is that Abram goes to Lot and gives him the choice of the best of the land (see vv. 8–13). He was able to allow his nephew to choose the best lands because, as I surmise, Abram was content with his relationship with the Holy One. The writer of Hebrews puts it this way: "Keep your life free from the love of money. *Be satisfied with what you have,* for he himself has said, *I will never leave you or abandon you.* Therefore, we may boldly say, The LORD is my helper; I will not be afraid. What can man do to me?" (Heb 13:5–6, italics added). Additionally, the psalmist writes: "Better a day in your courts than a thousand

---

thing. See W. E. Vine, *The Expanded Vine's Expository Dictionary of New Testament Words* (Minneapolis: Bethany House, 1984), 226.

39

anywhere else. I would rather stand at the threshold of the house of my God than live in the tents of wicked people" (Ps 84:10). Here is a proverb derived from my paternal grandfather, a man who truly learned the blessedness of contentment with God—it is better to be called to the abundance of poverty with God than to strive and acquire your own riches.

Know When to Release Others from Draining Relationships

Another important lesson we derive from this portion of Abram's life is knowing when to release yourself and others from draining relationships. From the context of the story, it is apparent that Abram had to separate from his nephew Lot. Particularly as leaders, it is incumbent on us to know when a relationship is no longer beneficial for the other person's good, as well as our own. All too often as pastor-leaders, we tend to go overboard with wayward sheep. Philip Keller in his classic work, *A Shepherd Looks at Psalm 23,* describes from the perspective of a shepherd the intricacies of the tough decisions shepherds have to make regarding wayward sheep. The decision to remove them from the flock is especially difficult but must be made because wayward sheep have influence on others to lead them into mischief. Titus 3 is clear: "But avoid foolish debates, genealogies, quarrels, and disputes about the law, because they are unprofitable and worthless. Reject a divisive person after a first and second warning. For you know that such a person has gone astray and is sinning; he is self-condemned" (Titus 3:9–11). I know it is not popular in many denominational circles to remove a person's membership from the church. However, I can attest from pastoral experiences that there are times when removing someone from the flock must be done; it is the right thing to do for the glory of God and the good of the church.

Principle #6: Leaders Must Learn to Care for the Community
One of the composite pictures we can draw from the life of Abraham is that he learned to care for the covenant community. All through his sojourning in the land of Canaan, Abraham's household continued to grow and multiply. Abraham, as the shepherd-leader and caretaker of the covenant community, displays four main functions: he is provider, protector, prophet (pastor), and prayer-warrior. What makes this so beautiful is that Abraham does not fulfill these duties alone—the Lord is the source of his supply.

1. **Provider:** Abraham was able to supply the daily sustenance of his people with his flocks, herds, substance, and relationship with the Almighty. As we study the entire life of Abraham, it becomes clear that the Lord is the Provider for Abraham, and in turn Abraham provides for all those in his household (see Gen 12–26 [esp. 22:14–19]).
2. **Protector:** As a military leader, Abraham fought for the covenant community to secure them in times of trouble (Gen 14:1–16).
3. **Prophet (Pastor):** Abraham functions as one who speaks for and represents the Almighty, first in his own home, second in his surrounding neighborhood/community, third in his place of ministry, and lastly in the public square (Gen 14:17–24; 20:7).
4. **Prayer-Warrior:** Abraham was able to be in the presence of the Lord, petitioning him for the needs of others (Gen 18:16–33).

Ultimately, in our circles of leadership, the Holy One is the source of our supply. The Lord, the great Shepherd of the sheep, is *protector, provider, prophet (pastor)*, and *prayer-warrior* for his flock. By way of extension, he calls us as leaders to function with him in caring for God's people. Additionally, he equips us as undershepherds to be his tangible representatives. He assigns to us these same four functions and charges his chosen with the responsibility to do his bidding for the sheep of his pasture (Ps 100:3). Without question, ministry leaders now and throughout the ages are called to care for the covenant community.[5]

Principle #7: Leaders Must Learn to Walk Righteously Before the Lord

This last principle is in some respects the most important of the group. The life of Abraham is hallmarked by his many encounters with God Almighty.[6] Genesis 17:1 is a template for not only Abraham's life but our lives as well. There the Most High says to Abram, "I am God Almighty. Live in my presence and be blameless."

Throughout the text of Scripture, God's people are called to be holy people who walk righteously. Speaking to Moses, the Lord commands him to "speak to the entire Israelite community and tell them: Be holy because I, the LORD your God, am holy" (Lev 19:1).[7] Importantly, we see in Leviticus God's instructions to the priest and the Levites to model holiness for the people.[8] The notion of God's people as examples of holiness is not left out in the New Testament—the call to holiness in both Testaments is equally proclaimed.

---

[5] See Lynn Anderson, *They Smell Like Sheep: Spiritual Leadership for the 21st Century* (West Monroe, LA: Howard, 1997).

[6] See Gen 12:1–9; 13:1–4, 14–18; 15:1–21; 17:1–22; 18:1–19; 21:33; 22:1–19.

[7] See also Lev 11:44–45; 20:7, 26; Deut 23:14.

[8] See Lev 8:1–36; 10:8–20; 21–22:16. A special note is provided in Lev 10:1–7, regarding the inappropriate presentation of offerings before the Lord and the grave consequences for doing what is unholy and not prescribed for leaders to do in the presence of the Lord—for the priests stand as examples to the flock regarding God's holiness and glory.

For instance, Yeshua in Matt 5:48 says, "Be perfect, therefore, as your heavenly Father is perfect." Following his Master's edict, Peter, in 1 Pet 1:14–16, references Lev 11:44–45 and 19:1–2: "for it is written, Be holy, because I am holy." Paul does the same in Eph 1:4 and Col 1:22, reminding the body of its call to holiness. Additionally, the New Testament attests to the reality that the Messiah's followers are *partakers* of the heavenly calling of Christ (Heb 3:1, 14) and are *participants* in his divine nature (2 Pet 1:4). On top of all of this, we have this admonition: "Pursue peace with everyone, and holiness—without it no one will see the Lord" (Heb 12:14).

Leaders of the community are called to uphold this calling of holiness to a much greater degree: "Not many should become teachers, my brothers, because you know that we will receive a stricter judgment" (Jas 3:1).[9] Peter's exhortation to the elders in 1 Pet 5:1–4 is a call to the highest standards of leadership, which the Messiah expects from his undershepherds. While this exhortation is positive, the opposite is to consider the results of leading God's people for all the wrong reasons. There would be much trepidation, and "weeping and wailing and the gnashing of teeth" (Matt 13:42).

THE KEY TO WALKING RIGHTEOUSLY

As mentioned above, this principle is likely the greatest of the list in that it brings together all the other principles. Like Abraham and virtually every other leader in God's kingdom, you have to be willing

---

[9]   John C. Maxwell, *The Maxwell Leadership Bible* (Nashville: Thomas Nelson, 2007), 1546, (Jas 3:1), notes that leaders and teachers receive a more intensified judgment from the Lord due to the intense responsibilities given to those who hold positions of leadership because leaders are specifically called to be Christ's examples to the flock as well as to the world at the "judgment seat of Christ." The notion that leaders are equal examples to the world is added by this author and not in Maxwell's original notation.

to *tabernacle* with the Holy One on the backside of the desert to learn these principles to the fullest extent. Do not fail in this area of calling! The Lord does his best work in the seasons of difficulty. In fact, Yeshua does many of his greatest acts of ministry in this remote environment. Think of the many times Yeshua is in a dry, desolate place performing miracles and the works of his Father! There, on one occasion, he feeds five thousand men, not counting women and children. On another occasion, there he feeds four thousand men, not counting women and children.

And it is there that you will learn to be intimate with him. There you will learn how to be mature, lacking nothing. There you will be prepared for a life of ministry by learning how to endure hardship and ridicule and how to hear when he calls out to you. You must learn to respond when the Messiah summons you to come and spend time with him so that you know him and he may endow you with power and authority to do the will of God. As Jesus modeled for us with his disciples, "Jesus went up the mountain and summoned those he wanted, and they came to him. He appointed twelve, whom he named apostles, to be with him, to send them out to preach, and to have authority to drive out demons" (Mark 3:13–14).

Conclusion

I hope it has been helpful to picture the call to Kingdom Leadership by viewing the life and calling of Abraham. To me, his life is the foundational template, not only for the faithful in general, but specifically for what it means to be a faithful leader to the bride of Christ. Viewing the different facets of Abraham's life provides rich material to understand what God requires of us. Matthew Y. Emerson uses the metaphor of a quilt to tie together many seams of thought that make up a solid biblical theology. In the same way,

Abraham's life is like an intricate quilt. Emerson's quilt metaphor can be understood as a picture of how the leadership principles of Abraham's life developed over the course of his years following the Almighty God.[10] He learns how to hear the voice of God when he leaves Ur of the Chaldees; he learns the lessons that can only be accomplished on the backside of the desert; and he learns to be a worshiper of God by calling on the name of the Lord, the Everlasting God. These moments of his life function as patches on the quilt, while his Immediate Radical Obedience Responses to the will of God are the seams that bind the quilt pieces together.

One thing that seems to be true of every great leader in God's economy is that they are called to the backside of the desert. Going there is a must. Neglecting to go there is a sure sign of potential failure.

The road to leadership in Christ's kingdom is not to be taken lightly. The road is simple, but the task is not easy. Often the Holy One calls us to places that are uncomfortable and even downright difficult. Nevertheless, he calls us and we must go where he leads.

As we traverse the remainder of this book, we will travel the road of developing a biblical theology of leadership, noting ideas, themes, and concepts that are biblical but in some ways possibly foreign to our reading of the text and our design for leadership. To be sure, our goal is to know his design for Kingdom Leadership and to know the voice of Yeshua, our Messiah and soon coming King.

---

[10]   Matthew Y. Emerson, *The Story of Scripture: An Introduction to Biblical Theology* (Nashville: B&H Academic, 2017), 16.

CHAPTER 3

The God News—Experiencing the Risen King

He was in the world, and the world
was created through him,
and yet the world did not recognize
him. He came to his own,
and his own people did not receive him. But to all who
did receive him, he gave them the right to
be children of God. . . .
The Word became flesh and dwelt among us.
We observed his glory, the glory
as the one and only Son
from the Father, full of
grace and truth.

John 1:10–12a, 14

The God News as I define it is the announcement and experiential presentation of the King in all his glory. Theologically and practically, the announcement includes his virgin birth, perfect life, death on the cross, his bodily resurrection with the demonstration of his transformative power (i.e., power to forgive sins), the promise of the Spirit, and his imminent return.

Our understanding of biblical leadership is wholly contingent on personally *experiencing* the transformative power of The God News and the presentation of King Jesus in all his glory. As some are no doubt thinking that there are other important facets of the gospel, such as Christ's ascension, let me be abundantly clear: what I mean by *experiential presentation* of the King is through both specific and natural revelation (Pss 19; 23 and 24; Rom 1:18–25; John 1:1–14; 14:15–24).

The God News is not an announcement that one simply hears and dismisses to return to life as before, like a person does after ordinary news surfaces. When my favorite professional football team, the San Francisco 49ers, was winning Super Bowls years ago, I was regularly elated that my team had once again won the big prize. It was great news for me as a fan. But the elation I experienced was short-lived, as I was almost immediately compelled to think of winning next year's championship. My team went through many years of drought where we did not win anything. The disappointment of losing soon erased the elation of the years of winning. This kind of ebb and flow is characteristic of the type of good news that is not transformative. Simply put, The God News is the transformative power of knowing Jesus. To know Jesus is to experience complete transformation that comes with his power and authority to wipe away all our sins and to holistically transform our lives (Matt 4:18–22; 28:16–20; John 20:18–23; Acts 3:18–20).

The God News, by its sheer nature, is eternally transformative. N. T. Wright articulates several conditions that characterize the transformative announcement of the gospel. The following points are taken from Wright's book, *Simply Good News*, with my augmentation:[1]

---

[1] For a complete understanding of Wright's concept of gospel as announcement, see N. T. Wright, *Simply Good News*, 1–7 (see introduction, n. 6). Points 1–3 are

1. The announcement comes in the larger context of the met-anarrative of life. That is the activity of God's saving grace and redemption that was put into place before creation (1 Pet 1:19–20 and Rev 13:8b, KJV) and is found in the life, death, burial, and resurrection of Jesus.
2. The announcement concerns something that has already happened—because of which everything will now be differ-ent. Life has been transformed.
3. The announcement has an intermediate period of waiting for the full consummation of the announcement to take effect.
4. Nevertheless, one can enjoy the benefits now, while antici-pating full consummation in the future. Jesus's good news was about heaven coming to earth.

When I think of The God News, like Wright's notion of announce-ment, we are talking about something that is personally experienced by the recipient. It is not simply heard; rather, what is heard is life-transforming. It must be *experienced* by the one to whom it is addressed, as expressed in Rom 10:17. The apostle Paul makes this abundantly clear in Col 1:13–14, which is one of the most concise and compelling announcements of the gospel in all his writings. Paul writes, "He [God] has rescued us from the dominion of darkness and transferred us into the kingdom of the Son he loves. In him we have redemption, the forgiveness of sins." Here Paul articulates this idea with action verbs that are personally experiential. God rescues and transfers; we are redeemed and forgiven. If we do not experience

drafted from Wright, while point 4 is drawn from ideas generated by Wright and George Eldon Ladd's notion of the *already-not-yet:* See George Eldon Ladd, *The Gospel of The Kingdom: Scriptural Studies in the Kingdom of God* (Grand Rapids: Eerdmans, 1959), 40–51.

The God News as described in Scripture, then I submit that we have not in truth experienced, nor truly heard, the announcement of the transformative power of the risen King.

The announcement and experiential nature of The God News inaugurated by Jesus as seen in Col 1:13–14 is as follows:

- God is the one who literally rescues us from sin, Satan, and death. The notion of rescue from the fall has its origins in Gen 3:15 and is one of the promises God makes throughout Scripture.[2] See also Ps 91:3, 15.
- God performs the act of transferring us from Satan's kingdom to the Kingdom of the Son whom he loves.
- God causes us to experience redemption (the purchase price of our transgressions).
- God provides the forgiveness of sins.

Experiencing God

Before we consider any further what it means to present The God News to others, we must first and foremost recognize that God is the initiator of any experiences with him. In the garden of Eden, the Holy One forms mankind out of dust. He brings what he formed to his mouth and breathes the breath of life into dirt "and dirt becomes a living soul" (Gen 3:7, ASV). In effect, God kisses dirt, and dirt becomes a living soul (picture mouth-to-mouth resuscitation). Adam's eyes flash open, and he is in the face of his Creator, Lord, and Lover of his soul. This initial experience between God and man is one of great intimacy between God and the object of his affection.

---

[2] See also Kaiser, *The Promise-Plan of God* (see introduction, n. 10).

50

The experience of God kissing dirt is like the intimacy between a mother and her newly born child—when the baby is handed to her for the first time and those little eyes open, a love pours out of the mother's heart that is like no other love on the planet. This act of intimacy between God and man is not a sterile experience, just as the intimacy between a mother and her newborn is not. Consequently, the presentation of the risen King cannot be sterile either.

Experiences with God

As we search through the scriptural record, a pattern of God leading humanity into experiences with him becomes prevalent. For example, God's relationship with each major patriarch starts with a God-initiated experience with the Almighty. After the early accounts of Genesis, God initiates an experience with Abram when he is in Ur of the Chaldees amidst a world of idol worshippers. Isaac has his first experience with the everlasting God when his father places him on the altar as a sacrifice. Later on, the Almighty appears to Isaac at Gerar and Beer-sheba. Jacob experiences the Almighty as he leaves Beer-sheba and comes to know him "in a certain place" (Gen 28:11). Jacob has the experience of wrestling with God, after which his name changes and he sees God face to face (Gen 32:24–30). Joseph experiences the Almighty in dreams (Gen 37) before rescuing his father's people.

In Exodus, God initiates experiences with Moses at Mt. Sinai (Exod 3:1–6). The Almighty hears the cries of his people, observes their misery, and promises to rescue them from all their oppressors (Exod 3:7–8). Throughout the remainder of the Old Testament, God continues to make himself known to leaders through his living Word, particularly the Torah, but often the most significant means he uses is direct experiences with him.

Joshua, the judges, Samuel, King David, and the prophets all had direct experiences with Yahweh. Isaiah is transported to the very throne room of the Holy One. There, a seraphim touches his mouth with a live coal from the altar of God and says, "Now that this has touched your lips, your iniquity is removed and your sins atoned for" (Isa 6:7b). In Jeremiah's case, the audible word of the Lord comes to him throughout his life. Similarly, Ezekiel experiences the Lord through the opening of the heavens; he experiences visions of the splendor of God, and the hand of the Lord is on him there (Ezek 1:1–3). Interestingly, never in all of these instances does Scripture record that the individuals experienced special revelation as we know it today or that God was made known to them as they read the Torah. This is not to devalue the written Word or any form of special revelation; Heb 1:1–3 is clear that the days of the prophets changed when Jesus came. Rather, it is necessary to come to terms with the fact that experiencing God is a form of special revelation. God is powerful enough to experientially present himself to believers, which in turn creates life-transforming effects. As modern-day followers of Jesus, we must remember to value God speaking to us as evidence of The God News! He uses his Word, other believers, natural revelation, and even his voice to teach us as we follow him, the glorious King.

The same pattern is made clear in the New Testament. Yeshua the Messiah, the highest form of special revelation, personally makes himself known to his disciples and eventually the whole world. He announces as God-Incarnate that he is the King and his kingdom is at hand; that is, heaven and earth's Lord is here to be experienced by all. Yeshua, by his personal presence, experientially presents the living God of Abraham.

Historically, there was a four-hundred-year famine of the voice of God when suddenly the Lord burst onto the scene. The archangel

Gabriel speaks to Zechariah and to a young virgin named Mary. Zechariah is silenced with muteness until the promise of John the Baptist is fulfilled—he is born, and Zechariah is filled with the Holy Spirit from personal experience. He openly prophesies the glories of God (Luke 1:67–79), preceding Christ himself.

The Most High then moves upon Mary, implanting the Holy Seed in her womb; she thereby gives birth to the Messiah. Angels preach to shepherds and tell them to go and see him, experientially presenting The God News of Yeshua's advent. As mentioned, the Messiah walks the earth as he ages, announcing that heaven has come to mankind—and to all who believe in him, he gives the power to become the children of God (John 1:1–14).

Many of the disciples were from Galilee and were considered unlearned, but surely they were sons of the Commandment; that is, they would have had to pass through the bar mitzvah and learn the Torah of Moses. It was when they experienced the Savior that they were transformed by his presence; Jesus himself was the literal announcement of the kingdom of heaven in their midst. These men (and women) are further transformed when they encounter the risen King. Mary Magdalene exclaims, "I have seen the Lord" (John 20:18). The Johannine Great Commission is reminiscent of the creation of Adam in the garden. There, in the garden, God kisses dirt, and dirt becomes a living soul and receives the breath of life. Similarly, the Lord Yeshua breaths into them and imparts the Holy Spirit to them (John 20:22), or at least proleptically they receive the Holy Spirit. Later on in the book of Acts, the text says, "When the Day of Pentecost had arrived, they were all together in one place . . . . Then they were all filled with the Holy Spirit and began to speak in different tongues, as the Spirit enabled them" (Acts 2:1, 4). The disciples experience him afresh and subsequently set the world on fire.

The Great Commission: Presenting the King

Each one of the original disciples took The God News of the risen King seriously and began sharing it near and far. They gave personal testimonies of the transformative power of Jesus of Nazareth. Thomas reportedly went to India testifying of his personal relationship with the King of glory.[3] Peter remained in Jerusalem and eventually traveled to Rome, where history records that he was martyred for his personal testimony of the risen King. He testified that he himself was an eyewitness, one who directly experienced the transformative power of the Messiah (1 Pet 5:1). The apostle Paul, who had a vast knowledge of the law of Moses, was of no effect for the Lord until he experienced the risen King on the road to Damascus (Acts 1:1–28:30). Based on that initial experience with his Lord, Paul is given the task of fulfilling the Great Commission, partially by penning well over half of the New Testament letters. The point is that, all through the Bible, God provides and presents us with experiences that are life-transforming.

The Great Commission—Experientially Presenting the Risen King Today

The apostle Peter reminds us that we, the chosen of God, have the same faith as he and the other apostles: "Simeon Peter, a servant and an apostle of Jesus Christ: To those who have received a faith equal to ours through the righteousness of our God and Savior Jesus Christ" (2 Pet 1:1). Paul goes on to remind us that we are recipients of "his divine power" and that we are "partakers of his divine nature" (2 Pet 1:3, 4). We come to be recipients and partakers of Christ, as those who possess the same faith as the original disciples,

---

[3] *Encyclopedia Britannica,* "St. Thomas," last modified February 19, 2022, http://www.britannica.com/biography/Saint-Thomas.

but only through personally experiencing salvation that comes in Christ Jesus alone! We, like Mary Magdalene and the apostle Paul, testify that we have seen the Lord. Our sins were nailed to the cross of Christ two thousand years ago, and we experienced the exchange of our sins for his sinlessness; our unrighteousness for his righteousness, our stench for his purity. In the same way we, like the apostles and the saints of old, are transformed by the cross and our experience of him personally, from which we announce and present The God News to a lost world—we proclaim with our lives that the King and the Kingdom are a present reality.

Experiential, in this case, means that we who have been transformed testify by words and deeds that we too have come to know him, that our lives have been made new (2 Cor 5:14–21); we proclaim with our lives that we have been rescued by Jesus, our sins forgiven, and that Christ has paid the price of our redemption (Col 1:13–14). It is not by our own inspiration that we testify and live for him—in fact, part of the transformative power of Christ is that no matter what we did in the past, we could not change ourselves to become who we are now. It is only when the Holy One of Israel opens hearts that lives can change. All of us should be able to make this claim.

To be frank, before I experienced The God News from the Messiah himself, my life was in shambles. I was hopelessly addicted to drugs and alcohol. When I was in the world with my friends, I would drink, get high, and preach. Most of the time my preaching to them was good entertainment; however, when I heard the transforming message of the Lord and he saved me, my life changed. From that point forward my friends would say, "Jones, there is something really different about you." They would tell me they could see the difference in me, and subsequently asked what happened. These are the moments I testified about my encounter with the risen King.

Now, my preaching was not mere entertainment. I preached a convincing message that the person of Jesus and his glory had intercepted my life. I told them of the day, the moment, the hour that he took the taste and desire for drugs and alcohol out of my mouth, with no withdrawal and no going back. They knew I had tried to quit using drugs and drinking a thousand times in the past, but this time they could tell the change was for real. It has been over thirty years now since I experienced The God News. And every chance he affords me, I testify of my personal experience of the truth that transforms.

We do not merely proclaim our subjective personal experience with the Risen King as the end-all, be-all. While I can see how testimony alone could be sufficient, there is so much more to gain with intentional studying of the Word also. After experiencing the risen King, we have the golden opportunity to fulfill the Great Commission, which proclaims, "Go, therefore, and make disciples of all nations, baptizing them in the name of the Father and of the Son and of the Holy Spirit, teaching them to observe everything I have commanded you. And remember, I am with you always, to the end of the age" (Matt 28:19–20). Particularly as leaders, we are called to be examples of the faith, as was our father, Abraham. We are to lead with skillful hands and integrity of heart like David the shepherd and articulate the full gospel like Paul.

The announcement and the experiential presentation of the King is especially the responsibility of those the Messiah calls to be in leadership. We hold the sacred task of not merely testifying about Jesus but making sure that others know all of God's Word. We must first maintain fidelity to the commandments found deeply embedded in the love and law of Christ. We are to teach the whole counsel of God from Genesis to Revelation, specifically but not limited to his virgin birth, perfect life, death on the cross, his bodily resurrection with the demonstration of his transformative power, the promise of the Spirit, and his imminent return.

Conclusion

The announcement and experiential presentation of the risen King is based upon our personal experience of him, as well as learning from the entirety of Scripture in order to teach and preach the whole counsel of God from Genesis to Revelation. It is made full when we engage in the process of making disciples of all nations. While it is inclusive of all of these elements, we must never forget that what we do as Kingdom Leaders is an act of worship. As his servants and children, we must reverently present him in honor of his majesty whenever and wherever the risen King is announced. Our posture in this process is one of loving subjugation and worship. Kingdom Leaders are called to be exemplars of the Messiah through personal testimony of how he has transformed us and how we live according to the calling he has sovereignly and graciously bestowed on us. Our leadership is to be patterned in a manner like the calling of Abraham; we are to obey him by teaching, preaching, and living the whole counsel of God (Gen 26:5). We are to walk this way from the beginning of our new life in him until our last breath.

We are ambassadors for him (2 Cor 5:20), and as such, we conduct business as officers of the royal court of our King. We are to be what Robert Smith Jr. calls "exegetical escorts" who introduce others experientially to a new relationship in the Messiah.[4] Smith references the queen of Sheba, who upon seeing the splendor of Solomon's kingdom returns home and introduces her people to the God of Abraham (1 Kgs 10:1–13). Similarly, Smith notes how the

---

[4]   Robert Smith Jr., *Doctrine That Dances* (Nashville: B&H, 2008).

woman at the well of Samaria functioned as an exegetical escort to those in her village. She calls them to come hear a man who has told her everything she has ever done. As the townspeople come to meet Jesus for themselves, they say, "We no longer believe because of what you said, since we have heard for ourselves and know that this really is the Savior of the world" (John 4:42). In the same way, Andrew functions as an exegetical escort to Peter, and Philip to Nathaniel, to announce and introduce him to the Messiah (John 1:37–51).

Additionally, Smith says our ministry as leaders and under shepherds is a ministry of reconciliation. Particularly, leaders are given the honorable task of being custodians who lead others to the throne room of God (Gal 3:24). Not only do we escort them into the presence of God, but we also are called to function like a "Spirit-empowered nanny" who helps to lead the newly born from milk to meat and from being a child to becoming a man—the once new believer is then able to be reproductive as one who has Christ's agency.[5]

We are God's people, his children—sons and daughters—called to be Kingdom Leaders (Jer 1:4–5; 31:33, 34; Ezek 36:28; John 1:12–13). As his people who are leaders, we must grasp how to lead the way through proclamation and demonstration of our deep and abiding relationship with him. Not only do we do this through presenting him via our testimony, we also make a proclamation of the announcement that heaven has come to mankind in the person of Christ Jesus and his kingdom. While preaching the whole counsel of God, leaders are specifically called to teach and proclaim the entire message of Christ—his suffering death on the cross, burial, resurrection from the dead, that he alone forgives sins, and his bodily return.

---

[5] Conversations with Robert Smith Jr., in light of his exegesis of the role of leaders as custodians, March 7, 2021.

In addition to our role as leaders, we must also consider our task as his messengers. The Holy One has uniquely fitted each one of us with particular gifts and tendencies to lead others for the purpose of fulfilling the biblical mandate. This requires us to deeply consider the foundation of our calling and all that accompanies that function. As leaders we are to be "passionate, not passive; fervent, not fake; bold but not brash."[6] As his representatives, we are to be dedicated to doing his works (John 14:12–14), thereby honoring his reputation. Moreover, we are to be grounded in Jesus so that when the word of the Lord comes, it is authenticated with signs and wonders, as produced by the Spirit. Through these signs the Master, the message, and the messenger are authenticated (Mark 16:14–20; Luke 24:44–53; Acts 2:1–3:21).[7] Therefore, we should humbly embrace presenting our experience with the risen King. While deeply appreciating the task of Kingdom Leadership with humble adoration, we should consider how we represent him as worshippers and proclaimers so we may be effective undershepherds of the grace of God.

---

[6] Words borrowed from R. Scott Pace, *Preaching by the Book: Developing and Delivering Text-Driven Sermons* (Nashville: B&H Academic, 2018), 16.

[7] The entire book of Acts is filled with authenticating signs, wonders, and miracles that bring glory and honor to the King and provide fulfillment to the Great Commission and verification of the ones sent.

CHAPTER 4

The God News—Chosen to Lead as Followers

*Jesus called them over and said to
them, "You know that those who are
regarded as rulers of the Gentiles lord
it over them, and those in
high positions act as tyrants over them. But it is not
so among you. On the contrary, whoever wants to
become great among you will be your servant,
and whoever wants to be first among you
will be a slave to all."*

Mark 10:42–44

*Follow me . . . and I will make you fish for people.
Immediately they left their nets and
followed him.*

Matthew 4:19–20

L eadership by "the book" requires a definition of leadership that
is comprehensive, one that, at a minimum, reaches for a solid
biblical theology of leadership. It must also include the involvement
of the triune God—Father, Son, and Holy Spirit—in the outworking
of leadership.

The remainder of this book will focus on defining a comprehensive concept of leadership that is reflective of the King and the Kingdom. To truly grasp a biblical understanding of leadership, we must first discover what a leader is in relation to Christ the King. Therefore, our working premise will be that Kingdom Leaders are incarnational followers of the King whom he appoints with authority, equips for service, and sends to influence all people to pursue the Father's will. These leaders display the active indwelling of the Holy Spirit in their personal lives and public ministries.

There are relatively few words spoken by Jesus on the subject of leadership. The ones we have are not only few but are truly paradoxical in nature. Much more is spoken by the Lord concerning followership than leadership. The call to follow the Messiah includes leaders and non-leaders alike. The call to follow Jesus is a strong imperative: "If anyone wants to follow after me, let him deny himself, take up his cross daily, and follow me" (Luke 9:23). In the larger scope of this text, Mark's Gospel includes, "For whoever wants to save his life will lose it, but whoever loses his life because of me and the gospel will save it" (Mark 8:35).[1] One thing is certain: being a follower in Christ's kingdom is not for the faint of heart. Paradoxically, leadership in the Kingdom is most characterized by following the Holy One. As the example of those who follow him reveals: "'Follow me,' he told them, 'and I will make you fish for people.' Immediately they left their nets and followed Him" (Matt 4:19). As we will discover, Kingdom Leadership is the new covenant paradigm for leadership. While this paradigm is based on the

---

[1]   In the Gospels, there are nineteen verses that specifically address Christ's edict to "Follow me." The notion of following him is extremely important. See James Strong, *The New Strong's Exhaustive Concordance of the Bible* (Nashville: Thomas Nelson, 1984), 370. Additionally, there are ten words in Greek that relate to the concept "to follow." The primary one in the Gospels (*akoloutheo*) is used seventy-seven times for following Christ. Vine, *Vine's Expository Dictionary* (see chap. 2, n. 4).

new covenant of Christ, it is built on the foundation first laid by Abraham as a follower of Yahweh.

Kingdom Leaders are those whom Christ has chosen for the task of leading his people; first and foremost, however, we are followers of the risen King. The individuals who are selected to be leaders are not chosen because they are special; rather, leaders are chosen by the Messiah for his purposes (Matt 4:18–22). Moreover, Kingdom Leaders are called to be undershepherds who are assigned the task of caring for the community of Spirit-filled believers, while remembering that we are forever the sheep of his pasture (Ps 100:3).

Kingdom Leaders are particularly called to model what it looks like to bear the renewed image of Christ and the indwelling of the Holy Spirit.[2] In sum, Kingdom Leaders (and all God's people, for that matter) are what I refer to as incarnational followers of Christ. What I intend by the phrase *incarnational followers* is a theology of incarnation that extends orthodox notions of the incarnation of Christ toward a theology of the incarnation of the Holy Spirit in the community of Spirit-filled believers.[3] The health of leadership

---

[2]   Much of my thesis for a theology for the incarnation of the Holy Spirit in the community of believers comes from the comprehensive work of Fee, *God's Empowering Presence* (see introduction, n. 12). Fee's work at minimum suggests that the empowering presence of the Holy Spirit in the community of believers should be made known in and through God's people.

[3]   Over the course of Christian history, there have been many debates and a rich body of literature developing the doctrine of the incarnation. My goal is not to rehash those valuable pieces of information. My goal is to provide a nuanced theological perspective of the Spirit-filled community as an [organic living organism] extension of Christ's work through the Holy Spirit in our present day—especially as it relates to leadership studies. For an in-depth study on the classical doctrine, see: Torrance, *Incarnation* (see chap. 1, n. 12). J. H. Walgrave, "Incarnation and Atonement" in *The Incarnation: Ecumenical Studies in the Nicene-Constantinopolitan Creed, A.D. 381,* ed. Thomas F. Torrance (London: Handsel Press, 1981), 148. James D. G. Dunn, "Incarnation," in *The Anchor Bible Dictionary,* ed. David Noel Freeman (New York: Doubleday, 1992). Karl Barth, *Church Dogmatics* IV, no. 1 (Edinburg: T&T Clark,

studies necessitates that our theology of the Spirit and our experience of the Spirit correspond more closely with the claims of the entire scriptural portrayal of the Holy Spirit. Regarding the giving of the Spirit as an integral part of the new covenant reality, God says:

> I will also sprinkle clean water on you, and you will be clean. I will cleanse you from all your impurities and all your idols. I will give you a new heart and put a new spirit within you; I will remove your heart of stone and give you a heart of flesh. I will place *my Spirit within* you and cause you to follow my statutes and carefully observe my ordinances. (Ezek 36:25–27, italics added)

God doesn't place his Spirit within us as a mystical force, but rather in the fullness of his all-encompassing presence in believers. Jesus came in the power and presence of the Spirit, and he sends us in the power and presence of the Spirit (John 20:22; Acts 2:1–13).[4]

Incarnational Followers of the King

Our faith as born-again believers begins with the acknowledgment of God in Christ "reconciling the world to himself" (John 3:1–16;

1965). Ross Langmead, "The Word Made Flesh: Towards an Incarnational Missiology" (PhD diss., American Society of Missiology Dissertation Series, University Press of America: Lanham, MD, August 2004).

[4] I realize that an argument for the incarnation of the Holy Spirit is a bold step and a full explanation of such a theology towards an incarnation of the Spirit exceeds the scope of this volume. My hope, however, is to provide enough of a biblical foundation to address my current subject matter of Christian leadership, and with all diligence address in full a theology of incarnation of the Holy Spirit in the community of Spirit-filled believers in a future volume. See Hastings, *Missional God, Missional Church* (see intro, n. 2). Hastings' thesis is not specifically about a theology of the

2 Cor 5:18–19). The expanse of a theology of the incarnation of the Spirit begins in the Old Testament promises that God himself would dwell among his people, that is, in the tabernacle and the temple (Exod 19:16–25; 40:34–38; 2 Chron 7:1–3).[5] Next the Holy One promises to dwell among his people as a person. John records, "And the Word became flesh, and dwelt among us, and we saw His glory, glory of the only begotten from the Father, full of grace and truth" (John 1:14, NASB1995). God tabernacles, that is, he pitches his tent in the form of human flesh as God incarnate, dwelling among us. Finally, as Jesus heads to the cross to purchase our full redemption, he promises to give the Holy Spirit, who will not only be with us but will "be in you" (John 14:16–17), which is in fulfillment of Ezekiel's articulation of the Holy One placing his Spirit in his people (Ezek 36:22–29a).

Powerfully, Christ's "be in you" is coupled with the promise that those who belong to Christ will not only do the works of Jesus but "greater works than these" (John 14:12–15). Moreover, the Holy One adds to his initial promise of the giving of the Holy Spirit; he says, "If anyone loves Me, he will keep My word; and My Father will love him, and We will come to him and make Our abode with him" (John 14:23, NASB1995). As the full complement of the Holy Writ, Jesus promises that his followers will be endowed, and I suggest incarnated, with the Holy Spirit in their inward parts, in that the fullness of the triune God takes up residence in his people.

New Testament scholar Alan R. Bandy posits that the main thrust of this passage is the giving of the Holy Spirit to the community of

---

incarnation of the Spirit. His work revolves around the inbreaking of the kingdom, shalom in the world, and a fully human existence for all of humanity. What is apparent in his writing is that his thesis cannot be accomplished without the church realizing a greater sense of the indwelling presence and power of the Holy Spirit.

[5]   See Kaiser, *The Promise-Plan of God* (see intro, n. 10).

Spirit-filled believers as the eschatological fulfillment of Old Testament promises. That is, the reality of the indwelling presence of the triune God, especially the incarnational presence of the Holy Spirit, is for the good of the individual but mostly for the good of the corporate body as living witnesses of the risen King.[6]

The impartation of the Holy Spirit into the life of the believer is made full by the promise that the triune God of Abraham will take up residence in his people. The Old Testament points to the fulfilled life experienced through the indwelling presence of the Holy Spirit as the life with God himself living in the community of believers. The life-giving Spirit indwells and does the internal work of circumcising the heart (Deut 30:6; Jer 4:4). Moreover, the indwelling/ incarnational presence of the Spirit fulfills what is lacking:

> I will make a new covenant with the house of Israel:
> After those days, says the Lord, *I will put my laws in their inward parts*, and write it on the table of their hearts; and I will be their God, and they will be my people. . . I will forgive their iniquity, and I will remember their sin no more . . . . I will also sprinkle clean water on you, and you will be clean. I will cleanse you from all your impurities and all your idols. I will give you a new heart and *put a new spirit within you;* I will remove your heart of stone and give you a heart of flesh. *I will place my Spirit within you* and cause you to follow my statutes and carefully observe my ordinances . . . you will be my people, and I will be your God. (Jer 31:33, 34b; Ezek 36:25–27, 28b, italics added)

---

6   Dialogue with Alan R. Bandy, Robert Hamblin, chair of Greek and New Testament exposition, New Orleans Baptist Theological Seminary, March 15, 2021.

The eminent scholar-pastor Claybon Lea Jr. posits that a theology of the incarnation of the Spirit can be built upon the first iteration of the *paraklete,* which is the concept of the Holy Spirit being humanity's advocate. Lea suggests that this first mention of a *paraklete* among us is seen in the Messiah's life with his disciples and the Jews of his day healing the sick, raising the dead, casting out demons, and performing other signs and wonders. Lea establishes that the second iteration of the incarnation of the Spirit can be seen in Jesus's promise of another *paraklete* of the same kind; "another Counselor. . . . He is the Spirit of truth. . . . But you do know him, because he remains *with* you and will be *in* you" (John 14:16–17). Third, Lea suggests that the giving of the Holy Spirit in the book of Acts (as a fulfillment of Old Testament promises) can be the basis for a full-orbed theology of the incarnation of the Holy Spirit in God's people in the present epoch.[7]

I suggest that a theology of the incarnation of the Spirit has its genesis in Jesus's high priestly prayer, seen in John 17. Throughout this chapter, Jesus adds foundational material to a theology of the incarnation of the Spirit. The following are highlights derived from this text:

- **Unity of glory:** The shared oneness between Father and Son is mirrored in *unity of glory and oneness* with the Son and the body of believers. Jesus says, "May they all be

---

[7]   Interview with Rev. Dr. Claybon Lea Jr., March 12, 2021. Dr. Lea is the pastor of Mount Calvary Baptist Church in Fairfield, CA. He is also a distinguished scholar whose dissertation, "The Hermeneutics of Desmond Tutu: Liberationist or Reconciliationist?" 2015, is a fascinating read. Additionally, Dr. Lea's insights into a theology of the incarnation of the Holy Spirit is well informed as a cancer survivor. He rightly posits that a complete study of a theology of the incarnation of the Holy Spirit is warranted. His thoughts and opinions are not to be taken as a full endorsement of a particular theological position on the matter.

> one, as you, Father, are in me and I am in you. May they also be in us, so that the world will know you sent me . . . I am in them and You are in Me" (21–23a).

- **Unity of purpose:** The Father, Son, and Spirit are *united in one goal* so that the Spirit-filled community of believers may be witnesses to the world. Jesus says, "I in them and you in me, so that they may be made completely one, that the world might know you have sent me and I have loved them as you have loved me" (John 17:23; cp. 6–10, 20–21. See also John 20:18–23).
- **Unity of love:** Between the Father, the Son, and the Spirit-filled community, the Father sent the Son and the love of the Father for them/us is the *same love* the Father has for the Son (23b–26).

Incarnational Presence of the Holy Spirit

The Johannine Great Commission is characterized by the risen King, at least in proleptic form, imparting the Holy Spirit into the disciples: "Jesus said to them again, 'Peace be with you. As the Father has sent me, I also send you.' After saying this, he breathed on them and said, 'Receive the Holy Spirit'" (John 20:21–22). Being given the Holy Spirit and being sent by Jesus as he was sent by the Father is a powerful picture of Kingdom leadership; the Lord empowers his people (by the Spirit) with the authority to forgive or retain the sins of others. The only way forgiveness of sins is given is by the authority and indwelling presence of the Holy Spirit.

Forgiveness of sins goes beyond person-to-person forgiveness, which is generally understood as forgiving others for wrongs done to you. While person-to-person forgiveness is important and true forgiveness is Spirit inspired, both Alan Bandy and I contend that the forgiveness spoken of and imparted to the disciples is greater than simple person-to-person forgiveness. We argue that what Christ means is more holistic in nature and is intended to function as a means to forgive others to the same degree Christ himself forgives. Bandy posits that "forgiveness is redemptive and restorative."[8] So the Johannine Great Commission can be itemized into the following parts (John 20:18–23):

1. It involves seeing the Lord (18).
2. It requires rejoicing in the reality of the risen King and the reception of his shalom (19, 20, 21).
3. We are sent by the Lord for gospel restoration of all others (21).
4. It is a reception of the Holy Spirit for life and ministry (22).
5. We are granted collective authority by the incarnational presence of the Holy Spirit to holistically forgive sins (23).

Incarnational Presence of the Holy Spirit for the Lifting of Humanity

To be clear, my argument for the incarnational presence of the Holy Spirit is not simply for the individual or his own good. And certainly I do not believe that we are transformed into Christ! What we become are Forgiven-Forgivers, not judges or arbiters of righteousness. We are transformed into what he intended us to be—the children and ambassadors of the Most High God. The following passages of Scripture discuss our role as new creations to be such Forgiven-Forgivers:

---

[8]   Dialogue with Bandy, Hamblin.

He was in the world, and the world was created through him, and yet the world did not recognize him. He came to his own, and his own people did not receive him. But to all who did receive him, he gave them the right to be children of God, to those who believe in his name, who were born, not of natural descent, or of the will of the flesh, or of the will of man, but of God. (John 1:10–14)

From now on, then, we do not know anyone from a worldly perspective. Even if we have known Christ from a worldly perspective, yet now we no longer know him this way. Therefore, if anyone is in Christ, he is a new creation; the old has passed away, and see, the new has come! Everything is from God, who has reconciled us to himself through Christ and has given us the ministry of reconciliation. That is, in Christ, God was reconciling the world to himself, not counting their trespasses against them, and he has committed the message of reconciliation to us.

Therefore, we are ambassadors for Christ since God is making his appeal through us. We plead on Christ's behalf, "Be reconciled to God." He made the one who did not know sin to be a sin offering for us, so that in him we might become the righteousness of God. (2 Cor 5:16–21)

Lauren K. Sierra, in a wonderful article, "The God Who Condescends: Leadership in the Gospel of John," suggests that the Gospel of John reveals Jesus's humility to lead in a lower order, a condescension. She claims, "The Creator became part of the created order, and the way in which he guided people was by willingly lowering himself into the human experience. As a father bends and lifts his child to see, so, too, John presents a God who stooped so people might be raised to life as his children."[9]

My position extends Sierra's argument in that the incarnational giving of the Holy Spirit is for the lifting and reconciling of all people back to a right relationship to God. Again taking our cue from Robert Smith, Kingdom Leaders are exegetical escorts, or what I refer to as *ambassadors of the pneumaton,* who lift and invite others into a new relationship with God through the presentation of The God News. Nearly every time Jesus engages with people, there is an opportunity for those he encounters to be lifted to his Father. Sierra refers to three pericopes where Jesus both condescends and lifts up those he is ministering to: the woman of Samaria, the man born blind, and Jesus's disciples at the Last Supper.

In the same way, our role, especially those who are called to incarnational leadership, follows the pattern of Christ by doing the works of Jesus (John 14:12).[10] Doing the works of Jesus is for the communal good of the Spirit-filled community. The works of Jesus are especially for people who are far from Christ—those in need of reconciliation and the forgiveness of sins. The risen King sends Kingdom Leaders in the power and presence of the indwelling Holy Spirit, so the world may be reconciled to him through a holistic call to repentance. Peter, filled with the incarnational presence, gives an indication of the purpose of the Spirit. He says, "Repent and be baptized, each of you, in the name of Jesus Christ for the forgiveness of your sins, and you will receive the gift of the Holy Spirit. For the promise is for you and your children, and for all who are far off, as many as the Lord our God will call" (Acts 2:38–41).

---

[9] Lauren K. Sierra, "The God who Condescends: Leadership in the Gospel of John," *Christian Education Journal* 18, no. 1 (April 2021), 60–61.

[10] See also the book of Acts 3:1–26; 5:12–16; 8:1–40; 10:1–48.

We Are Followers of the King (Akoloutheo)

The Greek term *akoloutheo*—to follow—has special meaning in the new covenant and special reference regarding what it means to follow Jesus. The term, because of its special use in relation to Jesus, etymologically evolved into the exclusive definition "to be a follower of Christ." It came to mean:[11]

- The follower, whom he calls to be a leader, leaves everything to go after Jesus and is characterized by deep internal attachment to Jesus.
- A strong sense of discipleship that is wholly found in relationship to Jesus; *akoloutheo* acquires a new content and impression.
- Essentially a religious gift. *Akoloutheo* means participation in the salvation offered in Jesus.
- Following Jesus exclusively involves fellowship of life, suffering, and fate with the Messiah, which arises only in union with the Messiah.
- To *akoloutheo* Jesus is not to be framed in conceptual or abstract notions; rather, what it is seeking is to express action and movement.

Jesus nuances the new covenant concept of leadership to express his unique formulation of Kingdom leadership. Jesus crafts leadership in his kingdom with a crystal-clear concept of what it means to be a leader; his brand of leadership must be exemplified by actions that are characteristically differentiated from secular forms of leadership. Christ's Kingdom leadership is what I refer to as

---

[11] List derived from trans. and ed. Gerhard Kittel and ed. Geoffrey W. Bromiley, *Theological Dictionary of the New Testament* (Grand Rapids: Eerdmans, 1995), 1:213–14.

leadership that is *contra-distinct*; that is, it is wholly differentiated from all other paradigms of leadership. Secular leaders, according to Jesus, often function as tyrants and lords over those they lead: "You know that those who are regarded as rulers of the Gentiles lord it over them, and those in high positions act as tyrants over them. But it is not so among you" (Mark 10:42b–43a). He goes on to exclaim that their form of leadership is to be contrary to that of the secular world (10:43b). Paradoxically, his paradigm of Kingdom leadership has an inverse function to it. The more one desires greatness, the more one becomes a servant to others (10:43c), and whoever wants more than this, particularly to be first, must become a "slave of all" (10:44). The highest form and example of following Jesus's leadership paradigm in his kingdom is martyrdom (10:45).[12]

Following Jesus Is All Encompassing

As the passages and list above suggest, the call to follow Jesus is no mere mental assent; it involves one's entire being. And as I have suggested, our response to the call of Jesus is *immediate radical obedience* to who he is as the King of the universe. The call to follow the risen King is the same call seen in the Old Testament call to follow Yahweh. Once again, following Jesus involves our whole being. Further, following the risen King is not merely a choice that one makes on his or her own terms—as though either I choose to follow him or I choose not to follow him. This is not voluntary service; it is compulsory servitude.

---

[12] Galen Wendell Jones, "A Theological Comparison Between Social Science Models and a Biblical Perspective of Servant Leadership" (PhD diss., The Southern Baptist Theological Seminary, May 2012).

The new covenant call to follow Jesus can be discovered in several action steps for what it means to follow Jesus with one's whole heart, mind, body and soul:[13]

1. **Follow me**: Engages one in a love relationship with the incarnate One, yet with the follower in total subjugation to the complete authority of King Jesus. The follower lives under the leadership of the *benevolent Master*.
2. **I will make you:** Jesus will cause complete transformation and an immediate status change in his followers as they become new creations (2 Cor 5:17). Additionally, transformation occurs in his followers over their lifetime of serving him through the process of sanctification (1 Thess 4:1–12; 5:23–24).
3. **Fishers of men**: He makes us new creations with new occupations and a new commitment to do as the King commands.
4. **Follower's response**: He leads us to an IROR to walk worthy of the calling of God.

Leadership that seeks to honor God must begin with following him. Rusty Ricketson comments, "I am a follower of Christ FIRST. Others may call me a leader, but my primary understanding of my place on the planet is to be a follower of Christ, wherever he may lead."[14] Ricketson's observation is the heartbeat of true Christian

---

[13] For a full complement of points 1–3, see Jim Putman, *Real-Life Discipleship: Building Churches That Make Disciples* (Colorado Springs: NavPress, 2010). See also, Jim Putman, Avery T. Willis Jr., Brandon Guidon, and Bill Krause, *Real-Life Discipleship Training Manual: Equipping Disciples Who Make Disciples* (Colorado Springs: NavPress, 2010), 25–37.

[14] For a full articulation of the follower-first thesis, see Rusty Ricketson, *Follower First: Rethinking Leading in the Church* (Cumming, GA: Heartworks, 2009), See also,

leadership. All too often the burden in leadership studies, including those of Christian leadership, is on the notion of a leader's influence on others. Anecdotally, we often say "he who thinks himself a leader and has no followers is merely out taking a walk." While this notion has bearing, the real onus is not on who is following us, but rather whom we are following—and what kind of follower we are. The true biblical notion of leadership is bound up in the paradoxical concept of following Christ Jesus. After all, Jesus's call to his disciples is, "If anyone wants to follow me, let him deny himself, take up his cross, and follow me" (Matt 16:24). The context of Jesus's statement is discovered in Matt 16:21–23. There our Lord points out the necessity for him to go to the city of Jerusalem and suffer many things and be killed by his own people. The Holy Spirit through Luke elaborates this point by picking up on the paradoxical nature of Jesus's edict; he adds that following Jesus is a daily process of self-denial and that one must take up the cross every day. Moreover, following Jesus involves losing one's own life: "For whoever wants to save his life will lose it, but whoever loses his life because of me will save it" (Luke 9:24).

The apostle Paul demonstrated through his life what it means to be a follower-leader of Jesus. We know from his life record that he suffered many things for the sake of his Lord. He boldly signifies what it means to be a Kingdom Leader when he admonishes the Corinthians, and by extension leaders today, saying, "Follow me as I follow Christ" (1 Cor 11:1). Following Christ implies that one spends time *with* Christ. Peter and John equally illustrate what it means to be follower-leaders in that it is clear that following the

Barbara Kellerman, *Followership: How Followers Are Creating Change and Changing Leaders* (Boston: Harvard Business Press, 2008). Ira Chaleff, *The Courageous Follower* (San Francisco: Barret-Koehler, 1995). Robert Kelley, *The Power of Followership* (New York: Doubleday Currency, 1992).

Lord means spending time *with* the Lord. Luke writes, "When they observed the boldness of Peter and John and realized that they were uneducated and untrained men, they were amazed and recognized that they had been *with* Jesus" (Acts 4:13, italics added). There is therefore a *withness* that authenticates our witness and is the identifying mark of true Kingdom Leadership.

The Transforming Withness of God

For those who are called as leaders, there is arguably nothing more important than the withness of God.[15] In some respects, the withness of God is the defining qualification for authentic Kingdom Leadership. Our foundational understanding of the withness of God can be discovered in the relationship God establishes through our father Abraham.

Withness of God in Covenant Relationship
The Holy One calls Abram to meet him in the desert so Abram may be *with* God, and there the Lord establishes his covenant with his chosen (Gen 12:1–9; 15:1–21). Abram follows the Lord's leading to the desert, where, for the rest of Abram's life, God is with him. One of the clearest pictures of the covenant relationship between God and Abram is that of Father to son. Abram spends twenty-four years being with God, learning what it means to be a son by his withness to God. Equally, in the process of learning withness, Abram comes to understand what it means to be a father even though he has not

---

[15] The ideas of "the withness of God" were developed from conversations with family therapist John Splinter, PhD. Splinter uses what he calls withness to teach fathers how to transmit family values to their children through the process of simply being with them. He suggests that when parents, particularly fathers, bond and share life with their children it functions as the chief means by which children most effectively develop value formation.

yet become one. Amazingly, through the process of following God and experiencing the withness of God, Abram is transformed and given the name Abraham so he will be what God destined him to be: the father of many nations. Abraham first meets God when he is seventy-five years old, and God makes himself clear to him fifteen years later:

> When Abram was ninety-nine years old, the Lord appeared to Abram and said to him, "I am El Shaddai. Walk in my ways and be blameless. I will establish my covenant between me and you, and I will make you exceedingly numerous." Abram threw himself on his face; and God spoke to him further, "As for me, this is *my covenant with* you: you shall be the father of a multitude of nations. And you shall no longer be called Abram, but your name shall be Abraham, for I will make you a father of a multitude of nations. I will make you fertile, and make nations of you; kings shall come forth from you. I will maintain my covenant between me and you, and your offspring to come, as an everlasting covenant throughout the ages, to be God to you and your offspring to come. (Gen 17:1–7, JSB, italics added)[16]

As I have made clear above, everyone whom God calls is required to spend time with him, and often in desert places. For instance, when God calls Isaac, he admonishes him to sojourn in the land of promise and gently reminds Isaac that he will be with him. God promises that he will surely bless Isaac as a form of covenant renewal from the covenant made with his father Abraham (Gen

---

[16]   Adele Berlin and Marc Zvi Brettler, eds. *The Jewish Study Bible: Jewish Publication Society TANAKH Translation* (New York: Oxford, 2004).

26:1–6). God appears to Isaac once again to remind him that the God of his father Abraham is with him (Gen 26:24). Both Jacob and Joseph experience the witness of God by becoming the father of the children of Israel and the leader of God's people in their initial descent into Egypt. Young David the shepherd boy spends many days and nights with God on the backside of the Judean wilderness preparing to become king of Israel. Jesus's disciples experience the witness of the Messiah while he tabernacles among them. As a matter of leadership development, Jesus intentionally sits with Peter, James, and John, as each one becomes a leader in the early Jesus movement. And lastly, all of the apostles, including Paul, experience the witness of God in the Person of the Holy Spirit as they are sent to evangelize to the world.

Witness is a quality that requires time and dedication; there is no substitute for time spent on your knees before the King of kings. Some practical tips to experience witness with God are:

- Spend time meditating and memorizing the Word. The more you engage with the Word of God, the more you understand who God is as Lord and Creator.
- Dedicate time to prayer. Time spent in communication with God functions in a similar way to time spent in communication with people on earth: communication binds us together!
- Open your eyes to what God has created. Look around you at the plants, the mountains, the ocean, or even the process of your friend expecting a child. God's creation proclaims his glory! The more you pay attention to the wonders he has created, the more likely you are to have a heart of worship before him.

- Commit yourself to a radical obedience response. Even when the call to obedience is difficult, remain faithful to what God has called you to do. When we walk with God in obedience, we learn more about his faithfulness and become more like him. As discussed earlier, time in the desert places with the Father are some of the most transformative experiences for our faith.

Conclusion

The call to Kingdom leadership in the days of the patriarchs, prophets, and kings was a call to be *with* God. The same is true of the call to Kingdom leadership in modern days. Because we believe that God's call to leadership is a consistent picture throughout the Scriptures, we can trust the God-ordained strategy of *withness* as a consistent model for us to follow as we engage in a relationship with Christ and one another. In addition, the call to Kingdom leadership rests on the foundation of what it truly means to be a follower of Jesus first.

The conviction that leadership in the Kingdom is an all-encompassing commitment to the lordship of Jesus is another foundational stone that sets the tone for relationship with the risen King. Anecdotally, we humbly embrace this by-the-book form of leadership. We are to bear in mind that what we do as Kingdom Leaders involves a healthy blend of the "science of leadership" with huge helpings of love for God, love for one another, and love for the others of society. As servants of Christ and slaves of our benevolent Master, we must deeply consider how to be with others in the same way we have been with Jesus, which when done with care manifests as an outward sign that we are faithful followers (Mark 10:43–44; 1 Cor 4:1–2). Leadership in this way hinges upon the indwelling presence of the Holy Spirit, as well as the objective evidence of love for one another (John 13:34–35) and a oneness of union described by Jesus in John 17:1–26. As we lead the people of God, our goal must be to lead in a humble demonstration of the Spirit and of power, so both the Spirit-filled community and nonbelievers alike will experience transformation that comes from the experience of Jesus's resurrection. Again, this requires the *withness* that only comes from being in the presence of the risen King.

CHAPTER 5

Appointed and Authorized by the King

Jesus came near and said to them, "All
authority has been given to
me in heaven and on earth. Go,
therefore, and make disciples
of all nations, baptizing them in the name of the
Father and of the Son and of the
Holy Spirit."

Matthew 28:18–20

There are three key characteristics within my definition of Kingdom leadership: all leaders are chosen, appointed, and authorized by the God of Heaven. All leaders in the Bible at some level are chosen for their role as leaders. A study of the Old Testament reveals that leadership is given by divine appointment. This includes bad and evil leaders such as Samuel's sons Joel and Abijah, as well as Israel's first king, King Saul (1 Sam 8:1–22). Equally in the New Testament, Jesus appoints leaders. At the risk of sounding redundant, the issue of calling or appointment to leadership has been sufficiently addressed in this volume. If more needs to be said regarding the biblical appointment and calling of leaders, I highly recommend reviewing some of the resources footnoted in those sections.

Authorized by the King

All authority is from God, who by his sovereign design established a clear created order. In Genesis 1, we see that God calls mankind to exercise dominion over the beasts of the field and the natural elements of the earth. He also bestows leadership and authority to mankind, both sacred and secular: "Let everyone submit to the governing authorities, since there is no authority except from God, and the authorities that exist are instituted by God" (Rom 13:1). It is from God's holy position of authority that he sends out his people to "make disciples of all nations," as quoted in the Great Commission. God passes on some of the authority in his kingdom to his followers. Although the term "authority" is helpful in the context of biblical leadership, God's definition of authority seems to be distinct from that of our culture today.

The Merriam-Webster dictionary defines authority as "power or right to give orders, make decisions, and enforce obedience," while adding that authority is vested in "power to influence or command thought, opinion or behavior."[1] The exercise of authority as defined above contrasts starkly with the biblical concept of authority.

To grasp the concept of authority in the context of Kingdom leadership, we need to begin the process of tying some strands together that make up the rope of Kingdom leadership. From what has been said in previous chapters, we need to draw in the ideas supporting the notions of withness and being incarnational followers of the risen King.

---

[1]   *Merriam-Webster Online,* s.v. "authority," accessed June 4, 2021, http://Merriam -Webster.com/dictionary/authority.

Once again, the life and call of Abraham personifies the life of Kingdom Leaders today. There is a need for Kingdom Leaders both to experience the witness that comes from a deep abiding relationship with God, as well as to discover what it means to be a follower of Christ. In tandem, these two aspects are the glue that holds Kingdom leadership together. Just as these are the most effective means parents use to transfer family values and an understanding of authority to their children, followership and witness with the Triune God are the most effective means for God to transfer his values to us and for leaders to know how to apply his authority for his mission. Lastly, a biblical understanding of authority in the Kingdom is given to, ascribed to, or bestowed upon those the Holy One chooses, and is never assumed or taken.

Kingdom Leadership of the King

Jesus alone, by virtue of his death and triumphant resurrection, possesses all authority in heaven and on earth (Matt 28:16–20; Rom 1:4). In the new covenant, Jesus clearly makes a grand distinction between the authority of worldly leaders and the authority of leaders in his kingdom. Jesus's edict, "not so with you" (Mark 10:43), demands that Kingdom Leaders be wholly differentiated from secular leadership. Interestingly, Jesus's conception of authority in leadership falls into what can be referred to as the biblical paradox.

Examples of biblical paradoxes include but are not limited to:

1. **Paradox of substitutionary atonement:** the life of the innocent for the death of the guilty (Gen 3:21).
2. **The finite wrestles with the infinite:** a man (Jacob, who is finite) wrestles with God (who is infinite) (Gen 32:24–30).

3. **God as man:** man as God or the dual nature of Christ Jesus the Son of God (Isa 7:14; 9:6–7; Matt 1:18–23).
4. **To save one's life is to lose life:** losing one's life is to save one's life (Matt 16:25; Luke 9:24).
5. **Death grants real life:** eternal life from death (John 3:14–16).
6. **Greatness through humility:** humility through servant-hood provides access to being the greatest in the kingdom of God (1 Pet 5:6).

Narry F. Santos suggests, "The biblical paradox is a self-contradictory rhetorical device used to jolt readers or hearers to chart a new course in thought and behavior. This new course of thought and behavior has risen from the concept that once stood in sharp contrast with one another, but when they are joined together a radically new premise of living emerges."[2] For instance, Matt 18:1–6 provides an example of the growing ideas surrounding the biblical paradox. In this text, the disciples ask Jesus how greatness is determined in his kingdom, in which greatness stands as a platform for authority and leadership. Jesus's answer to the question is framed in the form of a paradox. He calls a little child to himself and explains that "unless you turn and become *like little children*, you will never enter the kingdom of heaven. Therefore, whoever *humbles himself* like this child—this one is the greatest in the kingdom of heaven" (18:3–5, italics added). At minimum, Jesus's form of leadership is not only contradistinct; it is counterintuitive.

---

[2] For further insight into the notion of the biblical paradox, see also, Athol Dickson, *The Gospel According to Moses: What My Jewish Friends Taught Me about Jesus* (Grand Rapids: Brazos, 2003), 63–80. Dorothy A. Lee-Pollard, "Powerlessness as Power: A Key Emphasis in the Gospel of Mark," *Scottish Journal of Theology* 40, no. 2 (May 1987), 173–88. Narry F. Santos, *Slave of All: The Paradox of Authority and Servanthood in the Gospel of Mark* (New York: Sheffield Press, 2003).

The practical goal to be gleaned from Matt 18:1–6 is to strive to have the faith of a child. Jesus values humility over self-indulgent wisdom. It seems strange to imitate a child to be more fit for Kingdom leadership, but childlike qualities, such as the following, are what enable a person to be a leader in God's kingdom:

- One *turns* from what is common and secular to what is sacred and counterintuitive.
- One seeks to have a *position of heart* like children rather than common men.
- One seeks greatness through *humbling* himself.

Authority through Slavery and Servitude

In addition to the example of Matt 18:1–6, Jesus deepens our understanding of his paradoxical leadership through his wielding of power; Jesus does not demonstrate power in the exercise of his authority but rather in his ability to renounce the use of authority. Jesus transforms the traditional use of authority and power into acts of servitude and martyrdom (Matt 20:20–28; cp. Mark 10:42–45; Luke 22:24–30). Jesus employs the cross as the means to teach and equip the disciples to follow him. They must be ready, like him, to deny their own desires even to the point of giving their lives in death.

Here Jesus defines an inverse paradigm for Kingdom Leadership where the highest form of leadership is loss of life through martyrdom:[3]

---

[3] Galen Wendell Jones, "A Theological Comparison Between Social Science Models and a Biblical Perspective of Servant Leadership" (PhD diss., The Southern Baptist Theological Seminary, May 2012).

- **Level 1:** To be greatest is to be **a servant** = *diakonos,* as in one who serves in the diaconate, indicating subjection without the idea of bondage
- **Level 2:** To be first is to be the **slave of all** = *doulos,* as in one who is completely in subjection to the service of and owned by another. Most importantly, the *doulos* is distinguished as one owned by Yeshua the Lord—the benevolent Master
- **Level 3:** To be most like Jesus is to **give one's life** for the benevolent Master = *martyr,* one who bears witness by what he has seen or experienced and is willing to maintain his testimony to the point of death

To be a leader in Christ's kingdom is to serve—even to the point of death! To miss this reality is to miss the great call of Kingdom leadership altogether. Culture teaches that leaders are to dominate their followers, but the Bible teaches that leaders are to be humble and lowly. If Jesus came to serve and wash the feet of his followers, surely we can learn to lead our flocks from a posture of humility.

Seventy-Two as a Strategic Image of Kingdom Leadership
In the early part of Jesus's ministry, he called the disciples to follow him, and eventually gave them authority to continue God's plan of redemption for the human race (Matt 4:18–22). The twelve spent a few years of intimate time with him, seeing and experiencing Jesus's manner of life and teaching concerning The God News. Strategically over time, Jesus intentionally drew his disciples to himself in intimate relationship and gave them greater levels of authority to do his will: "Summoning the twelve disciples, [Jesus] gave them authority over unclean spirits, to drive out them out and to heal every disease and sickness" (Matt 10:1). Jesus repeats his process with

more disciples, thereby expanding his circle of intimate influence to wider and wider people groups. Luke's Gospel informs us that Jesus authorized seventy-two others to go beyond the villages of the lost tribes of Israel and to the Samaritans as well (see Luke 10:1–20).

Jesus's implementation of his strategic plan for world redemption reaches back to the Old Testament and moves forward to the present. The following tables emphasize the connections between God's execution of leadership and authority among his people from the Old Testament to the time of Jesus's teaching, and finally to the Spirit-led church.

The list below lays out the components and unique features of Yahweh's instructions to Moses for commissioning the numerous leaders in Exod 18:17–27 and the seventy elders in Num 11:24–25. There are striking similarities between God's plans for assigning leadership in the Old and New Testaments.

UNIQUE FEATURES OF LEADERSHIP AND AUTHORITY IN
EXODUS 18:17–27 AND NUMBERS 11: 24–25
   Exodus 18:17–27
   - Unspecified number of leaders chosen to share Moses's burden
   - Leaders are chosen and identified among the people who are able men, God-fearing, trustworthy, and who hate bribery.
   - They are to be educated in the Torah and to love and obey the Lord.
   - Leaders assigned to specified areas of responsibility with authority to adjudicate matters

Numbers 11:24–25
- Moses, according to the Lord's instructions, seeks seventy other elders known to him and the people to bear greater levels of leadership with him.
- Seventy elders presented in front of the tabernacle.
- The very presence of the Lord descends, takes the Spirit that is on Moses, and places it upon the seventy.
- The Spirit remains on them and they prophesy.

Kenneth Nehrbass and Jane Rhoades, in their article, "Jesus' Use of Experiential Learning in the Sending of the Seventy: Implications for Ministry Practicums," suggest that Jesus strategically sent out the seventy with his imparted authority as a direct representation from "both the table of nations in Genesis 10 and the Israelite elders in the Pentateuch. By this symbolic number Jesus was prompting his disciples to identify with Old Testament models of leadership that extend to all the nations. . . . They were no longer barely-educated laymen. They were God's emissaries to the world."[4] The dual process of spending time with Jesus and following his manner of life leads to Jesus's impartation of authority and the transformation of their lives into leaders who are useful for the worldwide mission of God.

Jesus's ultimate strategic plan for accomplishing redemption through Kingdom leadership can be discerned from a comparison of the Great Commission texts in the Gospels.

---

[4] Kenneth Nehrbass and Jane Rhoades, "Jesus' Use of Experiential Learning in the Sending of the Seventy: Implications for Ministry Practicums," *Christian Education Journal* 18, no. 1 (2021), 78.

JESUS'S STRATEGIC PLAN THROUGH SHARED KINGDOM
LEADERSHIP IN THE GREAT COMMISSION.

Similarities and differences between Great Commission texts:

	Matt 28:16–20	Mark 16:14–20	Luke 24:36–52	John 20:18–23
1.	Eleven together on the Mountain of Galilee according to Jesus's instructions.	Eleven together: Jesus rebukes the unbelieving.	Blesses the disciples/apostles with *shalom*.	Proclamation of the risen King by Mary and the other women.
2.	They all saw him—but some doubted.	Commissioned to preach The God News.	Shows them the marks of his crucifixion.	Eleven together in the upper room in Jerusalem.
3.	Full impartation of his authority to be emissaries.	Condemnation for the unbelievers among them.	Eats food to demonstrate he is not a mere aberration as some had supposed.	He blesses them with *shalom*.
4.	Commissions them to reach the *panta ta ethne*.	Jesus's miraculous signs and wonders accompany "all who believe."	Declares he is the fulfillment of the Promise in the Law–Prophets–Psalms.	Shows them the marks of his crucifixion.
5.	Authority to perform ordinances of the new covenant.	Apostles see the risen King ascend to heaven.	The risen King opens their minds to rightly perceive the Scriptures.	The apostles are "sent" by the risen King in the same way he was "sent by the Father."

	Matt 28:16–20	Mark 16:14–20	Luke 24:36–52	John 20:18–23
6.	Authority to teach complete compendium of The God News, beginning in Genesis.	Signs and wonders of the apostles will be authenticated by the risen Lord.	Commissions apostles to proclaim The God News.	The risen King in his own authority breathes the breath of the Holy Spirit into them—reminiscent of Gen 2:6–7.
7.	Called to remember the risen King is ever-present with them, and by extension is with Kingdom Leaders today.		The risen King assures them of the promise of the Holy Spirit according to the promise of God from the first Testament.	Authority to either forgive or not forgive the sins of others.

JESUS'S STRATEGIC PLAN THROUGH THE SPIRIT-FILLED
COMMUNITY

As precursors to the full promise of the Holy Spirit among God's people, the Risen King sends the promise of the Holy Spirit (Luke 24:49) and proleptically endows them with the Holy Spirit (John 20:22–23). The Holy Spirit changes so much for leaders in the New Testament. The following table focuses on the ways the Holy Spirit influences a change in the role of Kingdom Leaders.

The Book of Acts to the End of the Age:
- God's people (both male and female) experience the promise of the Holy Spirit through the speaking of other tongues (Acts 2:4).

- Everyone present heard The God News being spoken in their own languages—they heard the wonderful works of God (Acts 2:14).
- Signs, wonders, and the forgiveness of sins are performed by the apostles and all others who are filled with the Spirit (Acts 2:42–7:60).
- Experiential presentation of The God News spreads to the known world and beyond (Acts 8:1–28:28).
- The God News goes unhindered universally in the Spirit-filled community (Acts 28:30–31 and until the second coming of the Messiah).

Conclusion

Jesus provides two of the simplest and most profound commands to guide his people, particularly as it applies to Kingdom leadership. Jesus first admonishes us with the command *to love*, which is an invitation from the heart to be like our heavenly Father rather than an external command to be obeyed (Matt 22:37; cf. Lev 19:1–18). Through our love, we are to be examples to a lost world and to our fellow partners in Kingdom leadership. The second command relates to the importance of the Holy Spirit to fulfill his Kingdom purposes. This one, like the first, especially has bearing for Kingdom leadership in that we are to be continually filled with the Spirit (Eph 5:17–18), again setting the example for others to follow.[5]

As believers who are appointed and authorized by the King to serve his flock as leaders, we must remember that with authorization comes the call to (1) embrace an abiding withness with God, (2)

---

[5] For a full description of what Kingdom leadership looks like, see Ephesians 5. The Holy Spirit through the apostle Paul provides additional commentary and instructions for the Spirit-filled community to live by.

have an active faith like a child, and (3) embrace the biblical examples of appointed leadership. With these tools, Kingdom Leaders can seek to honor God, humbly serve their people, and lead with authority in the realm assigned to them.

> "Teacher, which command in the law is the greatest?" He said to *him*, "***Love* the Lord your God with *all your heart*, with *all your soul*, and with a*ll your mind*.** This is the greatest and most important command. The second is like it: *Love* your neighbor as yourself. All the Law and the Prophets depend on these two commands." (Matt 22:36–40, italics added)

> "I give you a new command: *Love one another. Just as I have loved you*, you are also *to love* one another. By this everyone will know that you are my disciples, *if* you *love one another.*" (John 13:34–35, italics added)

> "If you *love* me, you will *keep my commands*. And I will ask the Father, and he will give you *another Counselor* to be with you *forever*. He is the Spirit of truth. The world is unable to receive him because it doesn't see him or know him. But *you do know him*, because he *remains with you* and will *be in you.*" (John 14:15–17, italics added)

> "*Go*, therefore, and *make disciples* of all nations, baptizing them in the name of *the Father* and of *the Son* and of *the Holy Spirit*, teaching them to *observe everything* I have *commanded you*. And remember, *I am* with you always, to the end of the age." (Matt 28:19–20, italics added)

CHAPTER 6

Multiplying Kingdom Leadership

*And he himself gave some to be
apostles, some prophets, some
evangelists, some pastors and teachers, to equip the saints
for the work of the ministry, to build up the body of
Christ, until we all reach unity in the faith and
in the knowledge of God's Son.*

Ephesians 4:11–13a

On the surface, the notion of withness might seem to be an overly simplistic model for training leaders. While it is simple, it becomes more complex as one probes its depths of definition. We hear the anecdote that "more is caught than taught," and in some respect there is truth to this axiom. Training other leaders and equipping them for ministry is a task that requires dedication, life-on-life commitment, and an investment of time. It is not a simple commitment.

Withness, as I intend it to mean, extends beyond a withness with Christ to also include mentorship relationships. Young leaders need older, more experienced leaders to mold them into humble, focused, and godly servants to the Kingdom. Equipping leaders starts with a dedication to prayer on behalf of the ministry and the upcoming leader, but it doesn't end there. This chapter contains eight steps of discipleship to develop strong, healthy leaders.

It Starts with Prayer

Like many of you, I have had the privilege of serving in pastoral ministry for many years. One of the most difficult tasks I have found is to get people to be a praying church, not merely a church that prays. Most of the time churches pray in response to something or another that has happened—political fallout, natural disasters, a bona fide need for healing, or a host of other issues that are brought before the congregation. But the work of becoming a praying church with its people bathed in an ethos of prayer is more involved than you might think.

I venture to say, based on my experience, that few churches are "praying churches." And the work of transforming a church into a praying church is some of the most difficult work I have encountered in ministry. I challenge all my readers to conduct a straw poll—simply ask in your community or city if there is a church that is known as a praying church, a church that has a reputation as a place where prayer is the *modus operandi* and where they are known for having their prayers answered. I have no doubt that you will be both shocked and sadly amazed! Be sure to ask these questions to believers and nonbelievers alike if you really want to know the truth.

The environment of the church is to be founded on praying, and prayer is to be a lived experience as part of the church's way of life. That is, praying is to permeate our lives as Kingdom Leaders like rivers of living water flow from within (John 7:38).

Equipping Others: Creating an Ethos
of Leading by Following

Obviously, I am contending that prayer is one of the most, if not the most, important activities for the Spirit-filled community to engage in. Clearly, the biblical record establishes the veracity of prayer for God's people, and it especially establishes the role of leaders in this endeavor (e.g., 1 Sam 2:1–10; 2 Sam 7:18–29; 1 Kgs 8:14–9:14; John 17:1–26). One of the apostle Paul's most distinct qualities was his prayer life. All through his letters we are shown examples of his prayers.[1] It is therefore one of the chief responsibilities of Kingdom Leaders to demonstrate a lifestyle of prayer and to teach others in their sphere of influence to have one as well.

Equipping through an Ethos of Prayer

One of the most important tasks of a first-century rabbi was to teach his disciples to pray. Again, more is taught through observation and participation in this endeavor. The disciples learned to pray from watching their mentor, Jesus: "He was praying in a certain place, and when he finished, one of his disciples said to him, 'Lord, teach us to pray, just as John also taught his disciples'" (Luke 11:1). As the disciple observed his teacher's manner of life—in this case, prayer life—he was expected to mimic what he saw and thereby learn from doing what he saw his rabbi doing. Jesus did the same for his disciples. From the Gospels we discover that Jesus "often withdrew to deserted places and prayed" (Luke 5:16; see also 3:21–22; 6:12;

---

[1]   There are many fine references one can discover online or in a Bible bookstore. For example, Kevin Halloran's post, "A Complete List of the apostle Paul's Prayers in the Bible," kevinhalloran.net, February 8, 2014, https://www.kevinhalloran.net /the-apostle-pauls-prayers-in-the-bible/. D. A. Carson, *Praying with Paul: A Call to Spiritual Reformation* (Ada, MI: Baker Academic, 2014). Charles Haddon Spurgeon, *Lessons from the Apostle Paul's Prayers* (cross-points.org, 2018).

9:16, 29; 10:21; Matt 15:36; John 11:41–42; 12:28–29). He allowed his disciples to witness him in prayer and encouraged them to do as he did. Obviously, Jesus's prayer life was fruitful and displayed his reliance on his Father hearing his prayers. Moreover, Jesus, through prayer, heard from his Father and did what he saw his Father doing (John 5:19–21). In the same way Jesus modeled praying as part of his life for his disciples, so we too lead others by modeling prayer as a lifestyle for those we have charge over and providing opportunities for them to participate along with us.

Equipping Tomorrow's Leaders in Today's Church

As I have suggested, withness is the best way to become aware of the voice of God. It is by being near him that we become like him. In the same way, withness can apply in the context of discipleship. The leaders we surround ourselves with are those we begin to imitate. Withness in this sense is the primary means to lead others in a community of leadership. Yet, it is a withness with intentionality that is most effective. The following is a practical five-step process to equip others. The process is designed to be replicable and thereby ongoing. It should also be noted that this process can be short-lived or it can take months or years, depending on several factors.

A Paradigm for Equipping

Step 1: Leaders engage the function or activity of ministry they want others to emulate and learn. Simply, the leader "does" while others observe.

> *Evaluation:* Followers discuss what they have seen and heard, taking note of and learning from the leader's actions—both leader and peer learning.

Step 2: Leaders engage the function or activity of ministry; however, in this step, followers participate in the given ministry function or activity.

> *Evaluation:* Leaders and followers both learn from what they have observed. Importantly, leaders demonstrate lifelong learning skills in that they are also continuing to learn from their followers' involvement.

Step 3: Followers now lead in ministry function and activity while leaders assume the follower or helper role.

> *Evaluation:* Same as Step 2.

Step 4: Followers engage as leaders in ministry function and activity while leaders become observers.

> *Evaluation:* Peer-learning and evaluation of leaders.

Step 5: Those who were once followers now become leaders with others whom they are repeating the process with over and over again.

This structure is open to application in whatever ministry setting you serve. You can apply it to new pastors, youth or college students you are raising up to leadership, or adult volunteers in their sphere of influence. While the process listed above is a helpful skeleton, it is not very specific. Listed below are eight factors that influence the development of new leaders in ministry.

Eight Points for Effective Leader-Follower Formation

Practice Mentorship
Lead by demonstrating how you follow. It is crucial for leaders to maintain a teachable spirit. Every leader should have a few mentors

in their life from whom they learn. Except for Jesus, as he is God in the flesh, every good leader has others who have come before them from whom they are perpetually learning. This list of mentors should also be fluid and stratified. They should consist of people from church history you constantly learn from, like Charles Haddon Spurgeon or James Earl Massey. They should include people you know personally. For instance, I have several men and women I consistently call upon to learn from and who have entrance into my life. With these individuals, I have deep, personal, and abiding relationships that demonstrate that I have become dear to them for the sake of the gospel (1 Thess 2:8). Others are individuals I have had encounters with who have provided rich resources to my life and ministry. Be sure to include people who do not look like you, that is, they have a different ethnic makeup than your own, as well as a different Christian denomination than you. And lastly, have the courage to learn from those who are of the opposite gender.

The call to mentorship is twofold: as believers, we are called to be mentored, as well as offer mentorship to other people in our lives. Second Tim 2:2 says, "What you have heard from me in the presence of many witnesses, commit to faithful men who will be able to teach others also." As we learn and experience the power of being mentored, it is a calling to pass on the wisdom shared with us.

Learn to Ask Wise Open-Ended Questions
As leaders, we should ask questions that require more than a yes or no answer. In doing so, you lovingly compel followers to probe the Bible, life experience, and one another to discover the what, where, how, and why of life and ministry. Open-ended questions also lead them in learning how to hear from and rely on the Spirit, teaching them to discover solutions for themselves. While there is a place for yes and no questions, this method is the most effective means for

equipping others. Ask more open-ended questions than you answer, but always be ready to share wisely from your own life. Create an atmosphere where all parties share openly with one another what they have learned. And lastly, learn to ask wise follow-up questions that are application-oriented. The learner must be able to do something with—to apply—the information you shared with them.

DISCOVER LEADERS FROM VARIOUS LEVELS WITHIN THE CHURCH OR MINISTRY SETTING

As a shepherd, I constantly look for leaders at all levels of ministry—even young children. God is always at work developing and positioning his followers to take on leadership roles and functions. Look for youth and children who demonstrate influence and who have leadership potential. One thing I have discovered is that the young person who seems to be a troublemaker or who is always into something is often the one God is stirring to become an influencer among their peers. Be wise, draw them near, and do not be afraid to give them responsibility. I regularly apply Exodus 18 to fit my ministry context. We commission young people, with the guidance of their parents, to be evangelists, ministry leaders, young deacons and deaconesses, peer teachers, junior apostles, and prayer warriors. You will be surprised what a little coaxing, a little endowment of responsibility, and opportunities for young ones to lead others will do for the work of ministry. For a more formal model, see Jim Putman, *Church Is a Team Sport.*[2] I also look for seasoned married couples who will invest in young married couples. Then, the newly-invested-in young married couple is typically challenged to invest in another married couple, particularly nonbelievers. I allow all the aforementioned people access to senior leadership.

---

[2]   Jim Putman, *Church Is a Team Sport: A Championship Strategy for Doing Ministry Together* (Grand Rapids: Baker, 2008).

I also give lay members the opportunity to help shape my preaching series. For instance, if I am going to preach on a particular theme or book of the Bible for twelve weeks, I create teams of five to seven people from the congregation to help develop what I am going to preach for three to four weeks throughout the series. I give them the pericopes; I solicit their thoughts, prayers, and understanding of the material. I even allow them to come up with titles for the messages. As a man, there are thoughts and feelings that I can only get from a female perspective. Moreover, the thoughts, insights, and perspectives of an eight-months pregnant woman are simply priceless, and I could have never applied the text accordingly without her light. When I am really daring, I seek the input from nonbelievers. You will be surprised and refreshed when you gain their insights. We take way too much for granted and often miss the message of the text because we assume we know it or assume they cannot have a valid perspective. We also too often miss evangelistic opportunities by not having relationships with lost people. How can we reach them if we are incapable of hearing their valid questions about the faith?

DO NOT BE AFRAID TO ENLIST THE EXPERIENCE OF OTHERS WHO ARE MORE GIFTED THAN YOU

Ministry leadership is not for the faint of heart. Too often we fear what we cannot control. There will always be other leaders and people God has gifted with more talent, charisma, and ability than you. In light of this reality, never be afraid to enlist people who can be a blessing to you and the congregation. Exercise godly authority, be a blessing, and let others flourish. I have discovered that oftentimes, when there is a schism, it arises from senior leaders stifling the talents of those around them. Generally speaking, if you give room for others, God makes room for you. Loving people through the tough times of life and being with them as a shepherd is how God sustains you in ministry.

One of my former pastors, Bishop Bill McKinney, regularly introduced the congregation to other pastors and leaders who were more gifted than he was in certain areas. Bishop taught us that authority and security in ministry is not solely based on your ability to preach, or your talents and skills. Rather, your security in ministry is to be found in Christ's call to his service. If someone under you who is also called to serve in ministry has greater talent or oratory skills than you have, allow them to utilize their skills while you work on the gifts and talents God has blessed you with. He would often remark that we should walk firmly in the authority placed in us by Christ.

DEMAND LIFELONG LEARNING FROM THOSE YOU LEAD

Leading and lifelong learning go hand in hand. As suggested in the section on mentoring, make sure you have people from whom you are learning. Reading and learning from other Kingdom-minded leaders is fundamental to Kingdom leadership. Make sure to read authors who are different from you or who come from a different denomination. Read people who hold to different theological persuasions than what you are accustomed to in order to stretch your understanding and deepen your own convictions. Who are the people influencing you in life and ministry? By demonstrating an ongoing passion for learning, we inspire others to grow in their knowledge and foster a community of learners. This community of leaders will become a better team of leaders with a teachable spirit and active learning practices. Some active learning practices to consider are:

- Take a course in Bible storying or a foreign language.

- Lead those around you to go to conferences in preaching, church planting, or missions.
- Lead a mission trip.
- Simply put, look for and pursue opportunities to learn.

ALWAYS TAKE NOTES

The best leaders, in both sacred and secular fields, have one thing in common—they are always ready to write down thoughts, inspirations, or information they can use later. Note-taking sharpens the mind to listen for key applications and details of new information. It also enables you to retain information better—and the information you do not retain is written down for later review. Develop a habit of some form of notetaking. The best leaders keep a pen and writing pad with them at all times. There is a fundamental principle of learning that takes place when you physically write down information you do not want to lose. Teach those you lead, by example, to take notes.

CREATE PERSONAL STRATEGIC PLANS FOR LEADERSHIP DEVELOPMENT

There are many great resources for strategic planning that are readily accessible through a variety of sources. I have discovered that many strategic plans operate at the macro-organizational level. The reality is that the average church in America has seventy-five regular attendees on any given Sunday, according to the National Congregations Study (NCS), and that number has continued to decline in recent years.[3]

---

[3] More information on the National Congregations Study can be found at http://www.soc.duke.edu/natcong/. For a resource for up-to-date measures of the local church, see Thom Rainer: www.churchanswers.org.

The point for Kingdom leadership is not simply statistics of church attendance, though this is extremely important. The issue for our purposes is that with the turbulence of culture swirling around and within the church, it is incumbent on church leaders to create personal leadership development plans that involve comprehensive growth for leaders. The reality is, you simply cannot lead others where you have not gone or are not planning to go![4]

Those who aspire to be effective leaders should set a Kingdom leadership development plan that is personal and comprehensive. It should include virtually every aspect of one's life. Each area of planning should contain goals that are clearly executable and measurable and that others can hold one another accountable for. For example, Kingdom Leadership Plans could contain the following:

- A comprehensive (yet flexible) plan for family life:
  » For example, commit to being home by a certain time on weekdays.

- A personal and professional skill assessment and development:
  » This can be through a standardized test, a personality test, or a general assessment of those you work with.

---

[4] On the role of shepherd leadership, see W. Phillip Keller, *A Shepherd Looks at Psalm 23* (Grand Rapids: Zondervan, 2007); Timothy Z. Witmer, *The Shepherd Leader: Achieving Effective Shepherding in Your Church* (Phillipsburg, NJ: P&R, 2010); Daniel L. Akin and R. Scott Pace, *Pastoral Theology: Theological Foundations for Who a Pastor Is and What He Does* (Nashville: B&H Academic, 2017); H. B. Charles Jr., *On Pastoring: A Short Guide to Living, Leading, and Ministering as a Pastor* (Chicago: Moody, 2016); and Jimmy Dodd and Renaut van der Riet, *What Great Ministry Leaders Get Right: Six Core Competencies You Need to Succeed in Your Calling* (Chicago: Moody, 2021).

- Lifelong education:
    - » What educational goals do you want to accomplish? What goals could help you achieve a deeper understanding of your role in Kingdom leadership?
    - » This can be a class at your church, through a local seminary or university, or even an unrelated topic that enables you to practice learning a new skill.

- Health and wellness:
    - » Personally: this might look like a gym membership, a commitment to reach a step goal every day, or a certain number of hours you aim to sleep each night.
    - » Familially: your emotional wellness is very much attached to the condition of your family in your home. Make sure to include time investing in your family as a piece of your health and wellness goals.

- Clear and executable plans for how our lives can impact our community, church, and the world for the risen King!
    - » Set specific, achievable goals within your realm of ministry. An example might be a certain number of new church members or a metric of participation in a community event hosted by your church.

EVALUATE THE KINGDOM LEADERSHIP PROCESS

Every Kingdom Leader and every Kingdom ministry should have a means of defining, measuring, and evaluating Kingdom enterprise. These activities provide clear snapshots as well as medium- and long-term views of the whole terrain of the church. They afford leaders the vantage points to see where you are, where you are going, where course corrections need to be made, and what kind of routes are needed to get you where the King wants you to be.

The evaluation process functions like a topographical map. Kingdom leadership strategizing draws all the strands of biblical leadership together to help us see organically the development of the Spirit-filled community and show us the ways it can come to fruition. By extension of the ecological model, evaluation allows leaders to navigate the high peaks, low valleys, rivers, plains, and the varied human ecological spheres set before us. Solid evaluation fills leaders' understanding with insights from the past while providing clear discernment for the present and future. When evaluation and assessment are done with the guidance of the Holy Spirit, Kingdom leaders are provided spiritual insight for the journey ahead (John 16:12–13). Lastly, good evaluation practices allow leaders vantage points for the big picture of biblical leadership and an understanding of how the smaller parts of leadership fit into the larger whole.

Conclusion

In Kingdom leadership, Christ appoints and authorizes leaders to do his work in the world. For some, that is to "be apostles, some prophets, some evangelists, some pastors and teachers, to equip the saints for the work of the ministry, to build up the body of Christ, until we all reach unity in the faith and in the knowledge of God's Son" (Eph 4:11–13a). As leaders, we are to be faithful to our calling by investing in our communities and raising up new leaders through discipleship. In our own lives, mentorship and maintaining a teachable spirit are key. When we are faithful to develop ourselves and pour into the lives of others, it is powerful to watch God use the leaders he called to influence others for his Kingdom's sake.

CHAPTER 7

Sent to Send—Influence Others for the King

Jesus said to them again, "Peace to you.
As the Father has sent me, I also
send you."

John 20:21

All believers are called by the King and sent by him to further his kingdom. Some may utilize their roles as housewives, businesspeople, schoolteachers, lawyers, doctors, and so forth. To be sure, the Great Commission is the call of all who believe in Jesus. The core responsibilities of evangelism and disciple-making are for all of us. However, this chapter is directed toward those who walk in the calling of our father Abraham and who have a specific assignment to Kingdom Leadership: "And he himself gave some to be apostles, some prophets, some evangelists, some pastors and teachers, to equip the saints for the work of the ministry, to build up the body of Christ, until we all reach unity of the faith and the knowledge of God's Son" (Eph 4:12–13).

The Johannine Great Commission

The thrust of the Johannine Great Commission is discovered first in the transformative announcement of Mary Magdalene, "I have seen the Lord!" (John 20:18). One of the primary pieces of The God News is that we, like the disciples before us, can earnestly make the claim that we have seen the Lord! God's people and all who are called to him see the King as they see their sins nailed to the cross of Christ (Col 2:14; Gal 2:20).[1] The second and propelling thrust of the Johannine Great Commission comes from the all-important words of Jesus, "As the Father has sent me, I also send you" (John 20:21).

The Father Sent the Son

Jesus is the anointed man of promise, the seed of Abraham, the One sent from the Father who is the entire God News personified. After the fall of mankind, God promises to redeem man from the ravages of the fall. As discussed in earlier chapters, Gen 3:15 is the first place in Scripture where God makes a promise to undo the works of the fall, also known as the first messianic promise or the proto-euangelion. In fulfillment of Gen 3:15, God himself in the form of the Son appears to undo the ravages of the fall; as Scripture says,

---

[1] I owe this insight to the great African American pastor and theologian Dr. Ralph Douglas West, professor of ministry guidance at Baylor University Department of Religion in Waco, TX, and senior pastor of the Church Without Walls in Houston, TX. On the Bible's power of the individual to identify with the newness of life, John R. W. Stott suggests that it is discovered as one sees their sins nailed to the cross of Christ. See John R. W. Stott, *The Cross of Christ* (Downers Grove, IL: IVP, 1986), 254–64.

"The Son of God was made manifest to undo the works of the devil" (1 John 3:8).[2]

In an evangelical sense, Kingdom leadership is an extension of apostolic succession. Christ's followers, particularly Kingdom Leaders, are missionally sent by the King with the power and presence of the Holy Spirit to accomplish the will of the Father. Specifically, Christ commissioned the apostles in the first century, while leaders today follow in the direct line of succession as those who are called to fulfill the Great Commission. To be clear, I am not arguing for the Catholic Church's notion of apostolic succession where the pope is the vicar of Christ and the "holy bishops" alone stand in succession from the apostles. I am suggesting that Kingdom leadership flows from the beautiful heritage first given to those men and women who walked with Jesus. By virtue, The God News has spread throughout the ages by disciples and Kingdom Leaders who were sent in obedience to the calling of the risen King.

A Simple Biblical Theology of Sentness

This section is not intended to be a full theological treatise of the concept of sentness; rather, it is designed to provide the seed notions of how it pertains to orthodox Christian leadership. With that said, the theological notion of sentness runs the gamut of Scripture. Virtually every old covenant figure, from Noah to Abraham, from Jacob to Moses, to the anointed kings, and to the prophets, comes by way

---

[2] Biblical theology presents the promise of God as a consistent theme throughout Scripture beginning in Gen 3:15; see Allen P. Ross, *Creation and Blessing: A Guide to the Study and Exposition of Genesis* (Grand Rapids: Baker, 1998). Kaiser, *The Promise-Plan of God* (see introduction, n. 10). T. Desmond Alexander, *From Eden to the New Jerusalem: An Introduction to Biblical Theology* (Grand Rapids: Kregel Academic, 2008). Alexander, *The Servant King* (see introduction, n. 7).

of being sent by the Father for his purpose of redemption and reconciliation.[3] In fact, the notion of sentness in the Old Testament is one of the overriding concepts discovered therein.[4] The risen King fulfills all of God's messianic promises discovered in the first covenant. We especially see the risen King's fulfillment of the sent One as the embodiment of the significant figures who came as a precursor to Kingdom leadership.[5] The following are a few examples to illustrate the concept.

1. Moses is sent by Yahweh in more than one capacity. Moses embodies a full picture of sentness in that he figuratively illustrates for us the One who is Prophet, Shepherd, and King. Moses is sent to go before worldly authorities, rulers, and magistrates; he is sent as an undershepherd to faithfully lead and deliver God's people; as the leader of God's people, he is sent to exercise spiritual rulership as the servant-slave of Yahweh.

   Leadership Principle: unequivocally Christ is sent as the True Prophet, Shepherd, and King.

   » Christ Jesus is born as the complete fulfillment of each one of the offices. In the same way, Kingdom Leaders are sent to emulate Jesus by speaking prophetically for the Lord, and we are to shepherd

---

[3] For a list of old covenant persons, see Heb 11:1–40. There are other worthy examples of people God sent that provide fodder for what it means that the Father sent the Son. For instance, the faithful kings of Judah after the time of Solomon in the divided kingdom and Elijah and Elisha in the books of the Kings.

[4] The word *sent* and its cognates (*send, sending*) are used in the Old Testament approximately 689 times. Hand counted: Strong, *Strong's Concordance* (see chap. 4, n. 43), 935–37.

[5] For the foundational picture of Kingdom Leadership, see Abraham above.

God's people in meekness, as Moses did. Moreover, Christ the King demonstrates holiness, wisdom, and humility—similarly, every leader is called and sent to demonstrate holiness (Matt 5:48; 1 Pet 1:16; cp. Lev 11:44–45; 19:2; 20:7), wisdom (Prov 3:15–19; 4:7; 8:11–12; 16:16; Eph 1:17; Jas 1:5), and humility (1 Pet 5:6–9).

2. Joseph is sent by God as one who prefigures Christ's leadership as the slave who became royalty and the ruler who was a slave. He was exalted to leadership in Pharaoh's household and over the land of Egypt (Gen 41:37–57), after suffering through slavery in the home of Potiphar (39:1–20) and serving as a prisoner in the dungeons of Egypt (39:21–41:36). At first glance, we know that Joseph is sold into slavery by his brothers because of their jealousy that he is Jacob's favorite son. However, the greater theological purpose in Joseph as a type of Christ figure is in his function as the one who was sent to save and comfort his people. In essence, Scripture teaches that God sent Joseph as a savior of his people. In response to his brothers' query (thinking they sent him into slavery), Joseph responds, "Don't be afraid. . . . God planned it for good to bring about the present result—the survival *(salvation)* of many people. Therefore don't be afraid. I will take care of you and your children" (50:19b–21a). In a more expansive sense, Joseph represents potential salvation for the world in that he was sent by God to Egypt (a representation of the world) for deliverance from famine (41:46–42:38).

Leadership Principle: Christ is sent to save and deliver.

> » Christ Jesus is born the King; nevertheless in God's economy of redemption, Jesus traverses suffering and hardship as the Savior of the world (Heb 5:8), so we must learn to traverse hardship (2 Tim 2:3, 12; 1 Pet 4) as we walk the path of humility and righteousness. We must trust that Christ will raise us up to be used for his purpose of salvation and world redemption. It is our responsibility to experientially proclaim the goodness of The God News and respond to the Holy Spirit with an immediate radical obedience response.

3. In the same way Joseph was sent, David is sent by God to prefigure Christ's leadership as the Shepherd who became King and the King who is a Shepherd. David is called from caring for his father's sheep to become the shepherd-king of Israel. He is considered a man after God's heart (1 Sam 13:14) because of his intense faith in God, not his perfect walk with God. David has a sweet integrity in his heart toward God: "He [God] chose David his servant and took him from the sheep pens; / he brought him from tending ewes to be shepherd over his people Jacob— / over Israel, his inheritance. / He [David] shepherded them with a pure heart / and guided them with his skillful hands" (Ps 78:70–72).

Leadership Principle: Christ is sent to be Shepherd and King.

> » We learn to care for God's people the same way David learned to care for his father Jesse's sheep. Christ sends us to care for his people that we too will develop integrity of heart, practice keeping God's ways

112

(cp. John 14:15), and discover skillful shepherding practices. Some shepherding practices that prove beautifully applicable to a spiritual flock are feeding, providing for, protecting, consoling, and leading the sheep.

4. The overarching theme of the sentness in Isaiah's, Jeremiah's, and Ezekiel's prophetic writings is that the anointed One, who is the King, was sent to save. Isaiah helps us to understand that Yahweh sends Christ as the fulfillment of the Suffering Servant who saves his people from their sins.[6] Jeremiah and Ezekiel, in one sense, are sent to remind Israel of the consequences of corporate sin, but in another they are called to introduce the new covenant, eschatological salvation, and eventual restoration from exile. Clearly, the only one who can save is Christ Jesus the Lord! However, Kingdom Leaders are sent and commissioned by Christ as agents of reconciliation (2 Cor 5:17–21).

Leadership Principle: Christ is sent to suffer and save.

»   We learn to be Christ's servants through suffering in the same manner, so to speak, as he suffered (Col 1:24). Christ sends us as sheep among wolves (Matt 10:16; Luke 10:3) for the purpose of being witnesses and instruments of salvation. This is the model

---

[6]   The Servant Songs, also called the Servant Poems or the Songs of the Suffering Servant, are found in Isa 42:1–4; 49:1–6; 50:4–7; 52:13–53:12. Many evangelical scholars, this scholar included, consider Christ Jesus to be Yahweh's Suffering Servant—thereby fulfilling the messianic prophecies in Isaiah's lengthy discourse: "Servant of Yahweh: Gospels." Daniel G. Reid, ed., *The IVP Dictionary of The New Testament* (Downers Grove, IL: IVP, 2004), 1,011–14. Edward J. Young, *The Book of Isaiah: The English Text, with Introduction, Exposition, and Notes,* vol. 3 (Grand Rapids: Eerdmans, 1972), chaps. 40–66.

throughout the book of Acts. Suffering as Christ did is part of the beautifully mysterious paradox of the gospel; it is through suffering that joy is found and through humility that we will be exalted.

5. Ezra and Nehemiah are sent to rebuild the temple and the walls of Jerusalem. While Ezra is tangibly sent to rebuild the temple (Ezra 1–6:22), he is also sent to teach and reestablish the law of God. Ezra the scribe began to instruct the people in the law of the Lord (Ezra 7:6–10). Both Ezra and Nehemiah are sent to reconstruct the house of God and re-instruct the people of God. Nehemiah has a special burden for the people as he weeps over their condition in Jerusalem and is sent to unburden God's people (Neh 1:4–2:9).

Leadership Principle: In the ultimate sense, the Man Christ Jesus was sent by his Father as the true Temple and living Tabernacle, as well as the living Torah (John 1:1–14).

» Kingdom Leaders, in the same way God sent Ezra and Nehemiah, are sent by the risen King, as those who are indwelled by the triune God (John 14:15–23) to build and instruct the body of Christ (Matt 28:16–20). Nehemiah expressed his inward pain concerning the condition of the remnant in Jerusalem with tears and prayers. So, too, leaders today need to express godly concern for both God's people and the lost in humanity. We are called to pour out our souls and weep before the risen King as he wept over Jerusalem before his Father (Luke 19:41–44; Matt 23:37–39; see also Ps 55:1–7; Eccl 3:4; Joel 1:9; Jas 4:9).

The Risen King Sends Kingdom Leaders
"Jesus Has Forgiven Your Sins."

As Jesus begins the process of returning to the Father, he sends the Holy Spirit to be with and in his followers. He couches the giving of the Spirit of truth in the form of a statement: "If you love me, you will keep my commands. And I will ask the Father, and he will give you another Counselor, to be with you forever. He is the Spirit of truth. . . . He remains with you and will be in you" (John 14:15–16, 17c; see also Acts 1:8–2:12).

In the same way the Father sent the Son, the risen King sends Kingdom Leaders to do the same things he did. Jesus said, "Truly I tell you, the one who believes in me will also do the works that I do. And he will do *even greater works* than these, because I am going to the Father. Whatever you ask in my name, I will do it so that the Father may be glorified in the Son. If you ask me anything in my name, I will do it" (John 14:12–14). At minimum, the works we are to do are outlined in the works the King did while he was here. Kingdom Leaders are *called, equipped*, and *sent* to proclaim The God News with authority and power.

Kingdom Leaders are sent to continue the assignment God began before the foundation of the world: the work of redeeming mankind from the ravages of the fall and rescuing the lost (Col 1:13–14). The Johannine Commission uniquely reveals the missionary heart of God by sending the Son, and subsequently the Son sends his church (the *ecclesia*) to fulfill the mission of God.

There are several iterations to the missional sending of God:

1. God the Father (first Person—the triune God) sends Christ Jesus the preincarnate Lamb to be slain for the redemption

of sins before the foundation of the world: he is the redemption promised.

2. Christ the Son (second Person—the triune God) is the incarnate Lamb who is slain for the sins of the world in fulfillment of God's redemptive love on the cross of Calvary: he is redemption secured→ Christ the Son (the victorious risen King)—Lion of the Tribe of Judah—sends the Holy Spirit to indwell the *ecclesia*: redemption to the four corners of the earth.

3. God the Holy Spirit (third Person—the triune God) incarnates and indwells the Spirit-filled community as ambassadors of reconciliation: redemption already-not-yet.

This understanding of the commissioning and missional task of the Spirit-filled community has important implications. The mission of the risen King continues through our being commissioned, authorized, and indwelt by the Holy Spirit.[7] First we are partakers of the heavenly calling and of his divine nature; we live in the reality that we have been cleansed of our past sins.[8] Second, we are given his authority to do what he sends us to do. Third, we are to be in total subjection to him, not acting of our own volition. We are slaves of the benevolent Master—not independent contractors. Fourth, we are the sent ones who are led and accompanied by Jesus himself and the

---

[7]   Christopher J. H. Wright, *The Mission of God: Unlocking the Bible's Grand Narrative* (Downers Grove, IL: IVP Academic, 2006). Christopher J. H. Wright, *The Mission of God's People: A Biblical Theology of the Church's Mission* (Grand Rapids: Zondervan, 2010). Hastings, *Missional God, Missional Church* (see intro, n. 2).

[8]   The new covenant teaches that Christ followers are transformed into new creations (2 Cor 5:17) and that we are no longer sinners by nature (Romans 6), and that now in Christ we are partakers/participants of Christ, his Spirit, and his divine nature (e.g., Heb 3:1, 14; 6:4; 12:10; 2 Pet 1:3–4. Cleansing from past sins is supported by 2 Pet 1:9b; see also Acts 2:38; 3:19).

Spirit of truth. Lastly, we are enabled to exercise his authority as we obediently submit to his will, just as Christ submitted to his Father's will. Herein lies the paradox of our missional authority: "We find freedom insofar as we permit his enslavement of us; we bring life to others to the degree to which we give up our own for his Divine Will; and, we have authority and power in the measure to which we are willing to become helpless."[9]

Authority to Forgive Sins

Jesus, the risen King has conquered death, hell, and the grave. All who follow him are what I refer to as Forgiven-Forgivers. There are a host of Scriptures that attest to the paradoxical nature of the power of forgiveness. It is especially apparent as emanating from Christ's work on the cross. Romans 5 serves as a reference for the paradox of love and forgiveness for those who are undeserving of love and the forgiveness of sins. In this chapter, Paul writes, "For while we were still helpless, at the right time, Christ died for the ungodly. . . . But God proves his own love for us that while we were still sinners, Christ died for us" (Rom 5:6, 8). Christ died for the ungodly so that the ungodly may be forgiven and receive the right to the tree of life once again. As Forgiven-Forgivers we are compelled to be sheep among wolves; wise as serpents, yet, harmless as doves. Part of the essential nature of new covenant grace—what lies at its very heart of The God News—is the forgiveness that comes only through Jesus![10]

One part of the transformative nature of the proclamation of The God News is the forgiveness of sins. The proclamation of Peter

---

[9] Bruce Milne, *The Message of John,* The Bible Speaks Today, ed. John R. W. Stott (Downers Grove, IL: IVP, 1993), 299. Dorothy A. Lee-Pollard. "Powerlessness as Power: A Key Emphasis in the Gospel of Mark," *Scottish Journal of Theology* 2, no. 40 (1987): 173–88.

[10]   See Acts 8:22; Rom 4:7; Eph 4:32; Col 2:13; Jas 5:15; 1 John 2:12.

in Acts 2 is a prime example of the type of proclamation that I am suggesting. There he preaches that Jesus is the risen King and that he and many others are witnesses to the fulfillment of Scripture: "Therefore let all the house of Israel know with certainty that God has made this Jesus, whom you crucified, both Lord and Messiah" (Acts 2:36). The reply of those who heard him is telling: "'Brothers, what should we do?' Peter replied, 'Repent and be baptized, each one of you, in the name of Jesus Christ for the forgiveness of your sins'" (2:37–38). Three thousand people are added to the church in one fell swoop. The full impact of Peter's preaching is made clear with the following: "They [all the believers] devoted themselves to the apostles' teaching, to the fellowship, to the breaking of bread, and to prayer. Everyone was filled with awe, and many *wonders* and *signs* were being performed through the apostles" (2:42–43, italics added). Additionally, the Holy Spirit provides a prescription for the fullness of the proclamation of The God News from Acts 3, where Peter and John enter the temple at the time of afternoon prayer. Here we see that signs and wonders precede proclamation. A man lame from birth is healed through Peter and John by the authority they have been given from the risen King (3:1–10). Peter's proclamation (3:11–26) informs all who witnessed the demonstration of God's power that the man was healed by faith in Jesus's name (3:13–16). A key point from Peter's preaching of The God News is, "Therefore repent and turn back, *so that your sins may be wiped out*" (3:19, italics added). "God exalted him to his own right hand as Prince and Savior that he might bring Israel to repentance and forgive their sins. We are witnesses of these things, and so is the Holy Spirit, whom God has given to those who obey him" (Acts 5:31–32, NIV).

The forgiveness Jesus instituted in the Johannine Commission is the most radical revelation of the eternal vision of God the Father for restorative justice through the power of forgiveness the world has ever and will ever see.[11] By his authority he imparts to us the authority to do the works he did. It is the ultimate honor to be in the cadre of persons he uses to forgive the sins of others as we have been forgiven by God. "Therefore, as God's chosen ones, holy and dearly loved, put on compassion, kindness, humility, gentleness, and patience, bearing with one another and forgiving one another if anyone has a grievance against another. Just as the Lord has forgiven you, so you are also to forgive" (Col 3:12–13).

Whether we consider the authority to forgive others of their sins as Christ forgives us or whether we consider that forgiveness involves forgiving of original sin, it is a challenge to the body of Christ to radically reconsider our ideas regarding the Johannine Commission.[12] As the Father sent the Son to forgive sins, so too the Son sends us forth to forgive sins.[13] The binding and loosening of sins is founded upon the missional call from the Father to the Son and the Son to the corporate body of believers to experientially proclaim God's promise for the forgiveness of sins.

Milne suggests that proclamation is preaching only.[14] Yes, the preaching of The God News is transformative, but the proclamation of the gospel is based on words spoken and, of necessity, is coupled with demonstration of power in the authority of the Holy Spirit. The

---

[11]   For an impactful view of the extent of God's intention to use redeemed humanity for his purpose of restorative justice through forgiveness of sins personally as well as the corporate responsibility of the body of Christ, see Brian Zahnd, *Unconditional? The Call of Jesus to Radical Forgiveness* (Lake Mary, FL: Charisma House, 2010).

[12]   Forgiveness is part and parcel to the Lord's Prayer: "And forgive us our sins as we forgive others" (Matt 6:12). See also Zahnd, 29.

[13]   As a pattern for all those who follow the risen King, Jesus while he sojourned regularly forgave people their sins as an act of healing. For instance, see Matt 9:2; Luke 5:20–23; 6:37; 7:36–50.

[14]   On the argument that the act of binding and loosening of sins is only the result of preaching, see Milne, *The Message of John,* 299–300.

demonstration of God's power may come through signs and wonders accompanying biblical preaching (see Matt 28:16–20; Mark
16:14–20; Luke 24:45–53).

In the past forty years or so, it has become common knowledge
that the church in the West has been in decline. The Western church
has lost its place in society as the moral arbiter of culture, and her
influence has been relegated to the private spheres of life. What's
worse is that discipleship has been absorbed into citizenship.[15] In the
same forty years, the church in South America, China, and Africa
has been experiencing explosive growth.[16] One of the main differences between the two is that the emerging churches in the South
and East all hold that the proclamation of The God News is incom-
plete without signs and wonders following those who believe.[17] For
the parallel to hold, as the Father sent the Son to forgive sins, so the
Son sends his ambassadors, his church, to forgive the personal sins
of others by the power of the Holy Spirit within them. This must be
inclusive of those being sent with his authority to forgive sins in the
same way the Father sent the Son. The risen King's sending, particularly with the power and presence of the indwelling Holy Spirit, is
the continuation of missional sending.

Ambassadors of the Risen King

One of the prominent roles Kingdom Leaders engage in is ambassador of the risen King. As such, we are diplomatic agents of the highest

---

[15]   Marvin Olasky, *The Tragedy of American Compassion* (Wheaton, IL: Crossway, 2008).

[16]   https://juicyecumenism.com/2016/01/22/why-are-churches-developing
-world-so-vibrant/

[17]   Thomas Smith Kudoge, *I Need a Miracle* (Tema, Ghana West Africa: The
Conquerors Faith Chapel International, 2020). See also, Kudoge, *Identification:*

rank who are equipped, authorized, and sent with the indwelling of the Holy Spirit to conduct the business of God on earth. Additionally, as ambassadors of the risen King, we are granted all the rights, privileges, and power pertaining thereto. The apostle Paul in 2 Cor 5:20 confirms that believers are ministers of reconciliation. A wonderful modern example of what I am suggesting can be found in the testimony of Pastor Choco De Jesus.[18]

Second Corinthians 5:17–6:10 attests to our status as new creations and Christ ambassadors:

- Christ Jesus causes the old person to pass away while simultaneously making us new creations (17).
- Christ Jesus reconciles us to God through the forgiveness of our trespasses and has committed to us the ministry of reconciliation (18).
- Christ Jesus designates us as ambassadors (20a).
- In Christ Jesus we plead with humanity to be reconciled to God; working together with him, we refuse to receive the grace of God in vain so that the ministry of reconciliation will not be an occasion for offense (20b, c; 6:1).
- Christ Jesus determines the paradoxical nature of our ambassadorship (6:4–10).

The biblical foundation of becoming ambassadors of reconciliation originates from Ezek 36:23–28, where God promises what he will do to make us new creations:

Flying with The Eagle (Tema, Ghana West Africa:The Conquerors Faith Chapel International: 2020).

[18]   Todd Atkins and Ben Mandrell, "Episode 471: Choco de Jesus," *5 Leadership Questions* (podcast), August 5, 2021, https://leadership.lifeway.com/podcast-5lq/.

- God will sanctify his holy name among the nations so the nations will know that Yahweh is Lord God. He will demonstrate his holiness through us in their sight (36:23).
- God will gather his chosen from among the nations (36:24).
- God will cleanse his people from their impurities and idols (36:25).
- God will give his people *new hearts* and put a *new spirit* within them (36:26).
- God will place his Spirit within his people, in order that his people will follow his statutes and fully observe his ordinances (36:27).
  - » Jeremiah 31:33b says, "I will put my teaching within them and write it on their hearts. I will be their God, and they will be my people."[19]
- God will be the God of his chosen, and his chosen will be his people (36:28).

In summary, Kingdom Leaders are new creations called by the risen King for the purpose of announcing The God News so his kingdom may be extended far and wide. Both Ezekiel's prophecy in the old covenant and Paul's writings in the new covenant confirm that it has always been God's intention to send his church as new creations to be his ambassadors in a lost world. Jesus authorizes us to be his mouthpiece and make an appeal to others on his behalf to be made right with the Holy One. Additionally, we are commissioned by him as Forgiven-Forgivers and ambassadors who are authorized by the Spirit to be ministers of reconciliation in the spirit of meekness.

---

[19] For a full rendering of the notion of new creations and new birth, see Jer 31:33b and Ezek 34:11–37:24.

Conclusion

In all of Scripture, we see a picture of sentness. In the Old Testament narratives, the biblical leaders are sent to accomplish a purpose for the Kingdom of God, and ultimately each of these characters points to the coming figure of Christ, who will fulfill the Law. In the New Testament, we see Jesus live his life with authority to forgive sins and perform signs that display his power. Then, after Jesus is resurrected from the dead, the Holy Spirit comes down. The Holy Spirit becomes God in the members of the church, giving its members the authority to participate with God in the coming of his kingdom.

As believers who trust in Jesus and have access to the Holy Spirit in our souls, we have a responsibility to live as new creations and ambassadors of the King. We have a responsibility to be senders of new ambassadors as Christ has sent us. How are you participating in the Kingdom as a Forgiven-Forgiver and a discipler of other believers? Are you actively discipling other new creations to send them out as Paul did? Are you proclaiming the power of God with your tongue and in the way you walk in forgiveness with a lost world?

As ambassadors of the one true King, we must experientially proclaim God's promise for the forgiveness of sins and live with faith to see his power work wonders even today. The Holy Spirit in Acts is the same Holy Spirit who lives in the hearts of the modern church! Choose to live in faith that Christ Jesus is sending, equipping, and shaping you as a leader. And he is doing those things for you so you can contribute to the Kingdom by participating in what he is doing in the hearts of others. As a Kingdom Leader, do not miss it. Being an active ambassador for Christ, with humility and grace, is the greatest journey of all.

CHAPTER 8

Final Thoughts: Cultivating
Spirit-Led Kingdom Leaders

N ow that you have a foundation for a biblical understanding
of Kingdom leadership, what implications does this have for
those of us who are called to be servants of the risen King? What
is the trajectory for the church and society as a whole? As with any
paradigm of leadership, there ought to be a clear path for impacting
the world with the power of our Savior. This book should make us
rethink what it means to be in relationship with him on a personal
as well as a corporate level. Reflectively, I ask, has our view of
Jesus been refined to see him in the light of who he really is—the
"KING OF KINGS AND LORD OF LORDS" (Rev 19:16b)? Almost as
importantly, the question arises: Do I see my role as a Kingdom
Leader in light of who Jesus is and who I am as his servant and slave
(Mark 10:42–45)? My challenge to you is to ask God whether you
really walk in the footsteps of our father Abraham and the Messiah
with your whole soul.

Kingdom Leadership Involves My Whole Soul

The approach to leadership that I have outlined involves our whole
soul. That is, it should encompass the heart, the mind, and the body
(Deut 6:5–9; Matt 22:37–40). It should affect who we are spiritually.

Ask yourself: Who I am in my innermost self, where the Holy Spirit finds his dwelling place (John 14:17, 23)? Equally our approach to leadership should produce objective evidence of Christ's loving-kindness in how we live in relationship to one another in the church and in relationship to others who bear the *imago Dei* (Lev 19:18; cp. Matt 22:39; John 13:34–35; Heb 12:14).

Following Jesus with your whole soul involves the ongoing process of sanctification by way of sacrificial love and perseverance. As Kingdom Leaders, it is incumbent on us, by the guidance of the Holy Spirit, to actively engage in the process of growing in grace and maturity as servants, slaves, and children of the Most High God. As Paul explains in 1 Thessalonians 4, God desires for us to be sanctified and to grow in our brotherly affection for one another, which "you yourselves are taught by God to love one another. . . . But we encourage you, brothers and sisters, to do this even more" (1 Thess 4:9–10). Additionally, regarding the ongoing cultivation of our sanctification as Kingdom Leaders, Paul writes, "Now may the God of peace himself sanctify you completely. And may your whole spirit, soul, and body be kept sound and blameless at the coming of our Lord Jesus Christ" (1 Thess 5:23).[1]

Participants in the Divine Nature

One of the difficult concepts to grasp in the text of the new covenant is that all believers are participants in Christ's divine nature. The writer of Hebrews informs us that the reality of Kingdom citizenship

---

[1]   See also Heb 5:5–6:3. The clear expectation of this text is that as Kingdom Leaders, the Lord expects us to grow into spiritual maturity, that is, growing past the point of needing food for children to the place of being able to consume food for grown-ups. Moreover, the clear expectation, especially for leaders, is that we walk in the agency he provides by the living Word and the indwelling Spirit (also see Ezek 36:25–28).

is that we are holy, and as such we are participants in "the heavenly calling and have become partakers in Christ" (Heb 3:1, 14). Moreover, in 2 Peter 1:1–11, the apostle Peter speaks holistically concerning how we are to be cultivated as participants in God's divine nature. From this text, by direct and indirect implication, Peter asserts about Kingdom Leaders:

1. We are slaves [*doulos*] of Christ (Mark 10:44).
2. We have obtained a faith equal to the apostles through the righteousness of God and Christ (2 Pet 1:1).
3. Grace and peace are multiplied in us and through the knowledge of God and Jesus our Lord.
4. His divine power has provided everything we need for life and godly living through the knowledge of him; we are called by him, by his glory and goodness.
5. By his great and precious promise, we are partakers of his divine nature.
6. Through the process of ongoing sanctification, we are to make every effort to supplement our faith with goodness, knowledge, self-control, endurance, godliness, brotherly affection, and unconditional love (agape).
7. If we allow these ongoing/growing qualities to come to fruition, we will be fruitful in him.
8. By these, remembering that we have been purged of our sins, we will never stumble or fall.

Additionally, Peter reminds Kingdom Leaders that our leadership is hallmarked by the following from 1 Pet 5:1–4, 6:

- We are witnesses to the sufferings of Christ (see also John 20:18; Gal 2:20).

- We share in the glory of the Messiah that will be revealed in him (see also Col 3:1–4).
- We are to shepherd the flock of God (see also Ps 78:70–72).
- We are to willingly shepherd the flock without a heart of compulsion.
- We are not to lord our leadership over those who follow us (see also Mark 10:42–45).
- We are to be Christ's examples to our flocks.

Conclusion

Cultivation as Kingdom Leaders not only provides a platform for personal sanctification and growth in maturity but also emphasizes the command to take The God News to a lost and dying world. The aim of a leadership model founded on the example of Abraham requires that Kingdom Leaders be on mission for God so all people are blessed through our devotion to and mission for Christ. We are called to be heralds of The God News, exclaiming the life-transforming announcement that *Jesus has forgiven your sins. Repent, and you too can receive the gift of the Holy Spirit, NOW!* Cultivating Kingdom leadership provides a broad context where we help others to see the very heart of God's intention for his creation—"For God so loved the world that he gave his only begotten Son, and whosoever shall believe in Him shall not perish but they shall have everlasting life" (John 3:16, KJV).

Kingdom Leaders are on mission to be agents of reconciliation with all who bear the *imago Dei*. We are to become fruitful as exegetical escorts and disciple other true worshippers of the risen King. While we live out the calling to be exegetical escorts, we are commissioned to bring others into solidarity with the Spirit, not as lords but as servants. Those we help escort to the kingdom of God join us as those who experience *oneness* with the Father, the *withness* of Jesus, and *withness* of the Holy Spirit.

This description of Kingdom leadership is designed to be practical because the Scriptures concerning Kingdom leadership are practical. I wrote this work not only to provide a template for leadership but also for inspiration and transformation. These two go hand in hand. As we understand the biblical foundation for leadership, we understand more clearly the mission of God; the more the mission becomes a daily part of our lives, the more we are transformed by it. Kingdom leadership provides the framework for cultivation of our own lives as leaders, as well as a road map for developing others as Kingdom Leaders. In a practical sense, as we strive toward becoming more like our Lord, Kingdom leadership informs us of the adjustments necessary to stay on a healthy path toward Christlikeness.

Name and Subject Index

Scripture Index